CISTERCIAN STUDIES SERIES: NUMBER SIXTEEN

BERNARD OF CLAIRVAUX
AND
THE CISTERCIAN SPIRIT

CISTERCIAN STUDIES SERIES: NUMBER SIXTEEN

BERNARD OF CLAIRVAUX
AND
THE CISTERCIAN SPIRIT

by

JEAN LECLERCQ

translated by

CLAIRE LAVOIE

CISTERCIAN PUBLICATIONS

Kalamazoo, Michigan

1976

Originally published in French as
S. Bernard et l'esprit cistercien by
Editiones du Seuil, Collection Maitres spirituels Paris, 1966.

Cistercian Studies Series: ISBN 0-87907-800-6
This volume   Cloth: ISBN 0-87907-816-2
                   Paper: ISBN 0-87907-916-9

Library of Congress Catalog Card Number: 76-15487

© Cistercian Publications, Inc. 1976
1749 West Michigan - WMU
Kalamazoo, Michigan 49008

Ecclesiastical permission to publish this volume was granted
20 July 1973 by Bernard J. Flanagan, Bishop of Worcester.

Available in Europe and the Commonwealth from
A. R. Mowbray & Co Ltd. Osney Mead Oxford OX2 OEG

TABLE OF CONTENTS

FOREWORD TO THE ENGLISH EDITION

When this small book was published for the first time, a friend said to me: "Basically, you don't like St Bernard." To which I answered: "I hope I love him enough to be able to tell the truth about him." This spontaneous reaction hid no illusion however. Who can boast that he has penetrated the complete truth of a person, especially a man from the past, whose person and work do not compare with those of ordinary men like oneself? And yet without being able to pretend that one knows someone else well just because one has worked on his texts a long time, the fact alone that one has persevered in this study, and that one finds there a sustained and even a growing interest, shows that it is possible to sympathize with him.

There is nothing better than a long acquaintanceship—a lasting friendship, a love which has remained faithful—to help one not only better to perceive the limits of another, but also to accept him as more than he is; as he was, as God wanted him to be and loves him in eternity. Twenty-five years of friendship for St Bernard followed a period of distrust due to the reputation which he generally had among historians. Then ensued a time of enthusiasm which was indubitably excessive and is expressed in a book entitled *S. Bernard mystique*. Perhaps today's approach is balanced equally between those two previous attitudes: it can better show on which points and for what reasons one can admire St Bernard.

5

For the last fifteen years, the only list of publications which has appeared on St Bernard occupied almost as many pages as the text of the present volume.[1] All that work has not been in vain. But one has the right to believe that this con- stitutes only the basic research touching on the inner most being of Bernard, the sort one would be able to attain skim- ming the surface, as it were the shell, which are his texts and his actions. Beyond the particular situations in which he was involved, fields as diverse as doctrine, the reforms of his time, the reviving of monasticism, politics, he confronted the great problems which involve the whole life of man, especially if he is Christian: God, faith, the necessity of loving with all one's being, the resistance that one experiences sometimes from other egos, the Church and its government, society and its conflicts, culture, war.... Did he find solutions which were valid for him, for his contem- poraries, and which still today possess some relevance for us? The very fact that he is continually translated, read and studied would seem to indicate that.

But historical criticism and literary analysis are not sufficient to let us glimpse the depths of his being and of his message. Already there are attempts to explain them in the light of such infant disciplines as psychology, sociology and linguistics, which might possibly make use of computers. The task will be long and strewn with obstacles. But it will be fascinating. Bernard of Clairvaux is not an exhausted subject. Will the brief sketch which I have presented here stimulate the desire to examine him further? It would then have attained its purpose, which is not to satisfy our curiosity at all. St Bernard was one of those men through whom God revealed a little of who he is and what he does for men. While waiting for the final leap into the light, we will never know everything either about God, or about ourselves, or about those who serve as messengers between him and us: the image of God is never reflected completely in reality as

1. The bibliography to 1970 is given in E. Manning, *Bibliographie bernardine* (1957-1970). *Documentation cistercienne*, Vol. 6, Abbaye de Rochefort (Belgium) 1972, 81 pages. For the years following 1970, I have given indications in *St. Bernard in Our Times*, Oxford 1973, 20 pages.

an image is seen in a mirror; it remains an enigma. And it is already an important step to recognize the limits of the total effort we make to decipher it, and to accept them, in the joy of obscure certainty, in the hope of dazzling vision. This learned ignorance can only stimulate our desire: because he participated in it, the mystery of St Bernard can introduce us to the mystery of God.

Clervaux, July 1973

ST BERNARD AS MYSTERY

ST BERNARD WAS AND STILL IS a master of the spiritual life. The influence that he exercised both during his life and after it stands as sufficient proof of this: even in our own times, some new book about him appears every year. St Bernard is a saint. He was considered as such by most of his contemporaries, and the fact was proclaimed by a pope twenty-one years after his death. Does this mean that all of his actions were saintly? Let us apply to him the words once spoken to Newman with regard to St Cyril of Alexandria: "I know that Cyril is a saint, but nothing obliges me to assert that he was a saint in 412."

Bernard is one of those great men of whom it is difficult to write without either animosity or admiration—in other words, without passion. For he is both very great and very much a man. He is beyond us. We are, in turn, disconcerted, humbled, comforted, irritated. We appreciate the fact that he is human, very human, but it is painful to find him so much a man at one time, while he appears so much a saint in other circumstances. Did he ever achieve a synthesis of these contradictions? Can we?

What do we know about him? Among his contemporaries who left us some testimony, several were his adversaries, such as Abelard and his student Berengar. The latter even felt that he should resort to calumny in order to defend his master. But most witnesses were his disciples and admirers. The accounts that they have drawn up are enthusiastic, and

9

they tell us as much about the after-effects of St Bernard's life as of the life proper. One of these, Geoffrey of Auxerre, who had left Abelard's school to follow the Abbot of Clairvaux into the cloister, gathered together his recollections of Bernard, called *Fragmenta*, during the saint's lifetime but without his knowledge. These served as documents for the first biographer, William of Saint Thierry, who had been close to the Abbot Bernard. Since William also wrote without being able to consult the person involved—*nec ipso sciente*—his testimony with regard to Bernard's earlier years should be read with prudence. Moreover, he himself died five years before the saint whose legend he was constructing.

Another hagiographer, Arnaud de Bonneval, wrote the second book, and it fell to Geoffrey of Auxerre to complete the work by composing the next three books. All of this *First Life* is already an interpretation of Bernard's devotion to a cause which he had never ceased to serve: the excellence of monastic life in the Church, and especially the life at Clairvaux. Only a few rare witnesses like John of Salisbury, an aristocrat in that particular culture, could maintain their impartiality, if not indifference, in the matter. He was capable of admiring St Bernard as much as Abelard.

If St Bernard is a man before whom one must take a stand, it is because he embodies the very opposite of mediocrity. He is extraordinarily endowed by God and nothing that he does is ordinary. He excels in the most diverse areas, sometimes in areas that are positively opposed. Who can resolve such antinomy? Will his written work permit a resolution? Certainly we will have to refer to it. But here also we find a number of snares. Not so much because his immediate milieu assumed the right, as happened in other cases, to polish his style, add to his legacy or eliminate certain pieces: the problems concerning authenticity have been resolved. The greatest obstacle to an understanding of St Bernard, according to what he has said of himself, arises from the fact that he said nothing without writing it down and editing it. One of his most conspicuous gifts, however, was his literary skill, and the rhetoric which is evident in all that he dictated makes it difficult to distinguish the man from the artist. Perhaps the discovery of the sum total of his talent will cast new light on the intensity of his personality, a measure of the scope and duration of his radiating influence.

We can foresee that Bernard will remain a mystery. Nor do we attempt here to violate the secrets of history—do they belong to anyone but God?—but rather to identify, in the man himself, the true greatness by virtue of which he was and remains a guide for others. In him, everything was exceptional, even the human. This must be demonstrated. Undoubtedly this is why men of all times, including our own, have felt dazzled by his work and yet so close to him.

BERNARD AND HIS WORK

WHEN BERNARD WAS BORN in 1090 at the chateau Fontaines-les-Dijon, the West was in full evolution— something like what is happening in our own times. Population was increasing, the economy was developing, the authority of kings was becoming firmly established, that of the noblemen was becoming more organized, more civilized. Pope Gregory VII, who had died only five years before, had reinforced ecclesiastical power and given a new impulse to christian vitality. The so-called Gregorian Reform, drawing its name from him, was beginning to bear fruit. However, mentalities change more quickly than institutions, and perhaps these latter had not taken sufficiently into account the aspirations of the people. Widespread movements of public opinion were beginning to take shape everywhere in opposition to the hierarchy, and these gave birth to what were known as popular heresies. They taught and promised a purity which some individuals felt could only be made possible by breaking free from the laws of the Church, those which regulated morals as well as the faith itself. Thus Catharism grew.

Monasticism, weighed down by a long past history, bound to forms of existence related to an earlier economic and social order, was also in a state of crisis, but one that was on the way toward resolving itself. As a consequence, new religious institutions would rise up in which monks, hermits, clerics, and knights could spend themselves in ardent devotion to the service of God.

We should not forget the complexity of the religious life as
it then existed. It would falsify our perspectives by a fatal
oversimplification if we referred everything to two great
names: Cluny and Cîteaux. The former simply calls to mind
one of the witnesses to traditional monasticism as it was lived
at Gorze in Lorraine, at Hirsau, Saint Gall, Saint Emmeran
and elsewhere in the Empire, at Chaise-Dieu in Auvergne, at
Mont Majour in Provence, at Saint Victor de Marseille, at
Monte Cassino, and many places in France, Italy, Spain,
England and other countries. Like Cluny, some of these
abbeys were heads of congregations, sometimes grouping
together numerous monasteries into assorted federations or
affiliations whose juridical structures were supple and varied.
Their life was carried on according to the Rule of St Benedict,
but also and above all according to customs inherited from
the Carolingian Period. They were dressed in black, which
earned the religious of this particular set of observances the
title "black monks." The fervor, at Cluny and in many of
these communities, was real. But the institutions showed
signs of age: they were no longer adapted to the new forms
being assumed by social and economic structures.

In other milieux, after the last decade of the eleventh
century, there appeared a tendency toward returning to the
very sources of monastic life—Eastern texts, the Rule of St
Augustine, The Rule of St Benedict—in so far as these could
be known and interpreted. The aim of this search was a
greater simplicity of life, a more exacting kind of conventual
poverty. In compliance with these aspirations, there sprang
up communities and congregations of clerics who were known
as Canons Regular, as well as new types of monasteries and
orders. All of these were characterized by their habit of
unbleached cloth, used in its natural grey color. Such monks
were called "*grisei*" or, in contrast to the monks of the
ancient order, "white monks." For example, the group
called Canons Regular was comprised of Premonstratensians
and other "Augustinians," and, because clerics of this sort
officiated in the Lateran Church, the pope adopted the white

garment which has been retained up to our own times. Among those affiliated with the monks' group were the religious of Chartreuse and those of the Order of Cîteaux. Relations among all of these were varied, generally good. Many new foundations were helped by older ones. However, as the representatives of these diverse tendencies reflected on the reasons for their existence—the "innovators" enjoyed a prestige of which they could easily avail themselves and which others might envy—certain differences of opinion arose among some of them which provoked confrontations of ideas and even disputes which for more than half a century resulted in a literature of controversy. One of these quarrels placed several Cluniacs in opposition to several Cistercians.

Since the end of the eleventh century and up until 1118, the reigning Pope was an old monk from Cluny, Paschal II. Elected after him would be Gelasius II, an old monk from Monte Cassino who died at Cluny after a year's pontificate. They and their successors had to moderate many legal disputes between themselves and other sovereigns, between the emperor and the kings, and among kings. Within each state, the noblemen were often in conflict with one another and with their sovereign, while in certain towns, communes were being formed, and obtained or won immunities called franchises. In the midst of this fervent and restless society, in this world both crude and fragile, sensitive to beauty and capable of violence, there appears the great unexplained figure of Bernard de Fontaines, who became the voice of his era.

He had been preparing himself—or, more precisely, God had been preparing him, according to His own inscrutable designs—for twenty-two years. Since his youth, perhaps even since his childhood, he had demonstrated an amazing combination of temperament and grace. He was generous, but his fervor carried him, in turn, toward wordly realities and toward the demands of God. We know nothing of his education, but the results indicate that it was excellent. We can guess that it was oriented toward literature rather than dialectic, that science of reasoning which attracted so many

young minds in the cities at that time—the urban schools
were in the process of elaborating what would later become
"scholasticism." Unlike his brothers and cousins, Bernard
was not a soldier, nor was he a cleric. Was he looking for
someone, something? Would he find his own balance? Was
he fragile and unstable? He was energetic, tenacious, able to
sustain long-term efforts. John of Salisbury would later describe him as "efficient." At the same time, he was shy. He
was sensitive and, though we could not call him sickly—for
he appeared healthy—he was already acquainted with illness,
perhaps paying for the excessive fervor spent in his moments
of activity, of intense effort, both interior and exterior, with
his periods of fatigue.

God was fashioning him, and he did not resist. He waited
and, already, he struggled. At twenty years old, and
probably even earlier, he felt called to make a total gift of
himself. One last choice succeeded in liberating him: in face
of the option to study in some great city, he preferred the
seclusion of the cloister. But he did not want to enter alone.
He persuaded his uncle, his brothers, his cousins and his
friends. And this group of about thirty adult novices, already
seasoned in life's struggles, came to present themselves at a
monastery founded twelve years earlier, known for its
austerities, in order to embrace its purpose of remaining far
from the society of men. This monastery was Cîteaux. Thus
they manifested in a very striking way their will to imitate
Jesus Christ and, the better to participate in the renunciation
and joy of the mystery of his death and resurrection, they
chose to arrive, according to Geoffrey of Auxerre, "shortly
before Easter."

Bernard and his companions spent their novitiate, uttered
their profession, and, three years after their entrance, their
leader, now twenty-five years of age, was sent to found
Clairvaux in Champagne. He became the abbot, that is the
father, of his brothers and his elders, and he devoted himself
to their formation and to the material establishment of his
monastery. He seldom went out but he drew others to
himself. William of Saint Thierry, a great theologian of that

time, came to visit him. Above all, new recruits abounded.
Three years after its own debut, Clairvaux founded its first
daughter-house, Trois-Fontaines, and the following year a
second, Fontenay. During a space of thirty years, Clairvaux's
expansion proceeded in an average rhythm of two foundations
per year. At his death in 1153, Bernard would be the father
of seventy communities, besides those which were affiliated
by him. The total would come to one hundred and sixty-four,
almost half the entire Order of Cîteaux. He was beginning to
animate this vast body while continuing to study and improve
his own mind. He was urged to write and he did so. By his
thirtieth year, in his first works, he already showed himself to
be in full possession of his influential powers. Henceforth,
there would be hardly any evolution in his character or in his
actions, in his thought or in his style. At this point, what
kind of a man was he? What had he done with the resources
of his own nature bestowed on him by God?

Bernard's Gifts

It is difficult to say, so varied were the gifts and so intensified by grace. The general impression is one of extreme
vitality. Such terms as dynamism and even magnetism have
been applied to him. Certainly there was a great deal of
courage in him, and it seems probable that he also retained
traces of shyness. There was in him both violence and
gentleness. He was virile and maternal. His intelligence was
eager, quick, able to grasp seeds of learning everywhere and
then make them grow in his own way. He had an acute
sense of observation, a vivid imagination, an exceptional
capacity for feeling and he was easily moved, a burning
heart, generous in charity, passionate in disputation. It is
evident that his years at Cîteaux and his first years in the
abbatial office contributed to the deterioration of his health. It
is difficult to diagnose the particular illness which afflicted
him. The most concise health report that we have on him is
perhaps not entirely free of rhetoric. It is found in a letter
addressed to his second biographer, Arnaud de Bonneval,

and its authenticity is questionable. Sickness could become a literary theme. From the descriptions of his condition set forth by his contemporaries and by Bernard himself, we could possibly recognize a chronic gastritis developing into a pyloric ulcer, accompanied by neuralgia, stomach spasms and cramps, intestinal difficulties, and asthenia. None of these ailments was fatal, nor perhaps even serious. But taken together they explain that emaciated look, the pale countenance and flushed cheeks that Geoffrey of Auxerre has depicted. Often, if not habitually, Bernard felt overwhelmed, exhausted. During certain periods he suffered intensely and became a burden to himself and others, and this humiliating physical condition, known to all, would have given him the right to certain dispensations. But it was in this very state that he studied, worked, traveled, made foundations, and intervened in the direction of souls and in the affairs of the Church. His weakness was coupled with energy, the frailty of the organism with strength of will.

As for those gifts which "adorned the spirit"—according to an expression that he liked—those talents which he had received in abundance and brought to fruition: in what order can we approach them? For they are simply different aspects of one intense personality. Bernard was a poet. His way of looking at the world made him a creator. He added to what he saw, transformed what he contemplated, discovered something beyond the obvious. He penetrated to the very designs of God whose light, shining through him, embellished the objects apprehended by his senses. Under the influence of unchecked prejudices or following upon a superficial reading, a certain suspicion and even a pessimism toward nature has been attributed to Bernard. But a meticulous examination of his work, from this point of view, reveals an abundance of picturesque symbols. We cannot attempt to analyse them here and must limit ourselves to verifying their existence. Examples of fauna are predominant over those of flora; as if Bernard had a natural preference for what is animated. Nevertheless, nothing is missing from the scene. The elements, the stars and the seasons, rocks, plants and animals are often mentioned, and it is in his sermons that allusions of this sort are most frequent. In all of this, Bernard belongs to a tradition which reaches back to Pliny and the ancient naturalists through the Fathers of the Church and St Isidore of Seville, to the authors of the medieval bestiaries and lapidaries. The Bible, especially, was his school of piety. From it he learned admiration. It taught him that the original order of things, after having been unsettled by sin, can and must be restored in the Lord Jesus. *Mirum opus naturae!* "How marvelous is the working of nature!" he exclaims in Letter 72. And he applied this principle to the graceful flight of the birds and the speed of the quadriga, both of these examples of value in encouraging those who would follow Christ. He was truly inclined toward the book of nature, which he speaks of in the ninth of his miscellaneous Sermons. Here he found moral lessons and salutary comparisons. And these artificial themes, which could have furnished mere faded images, were expressed with a freshness, occasionally a fondness, which is an indication of his good humor and mental health.

Bernard was an artist. He needed beauty. He brought it into existence, but he was also selective. He wanted it pure and simple like the God whom it was meant to reflect. In this area, we must guard against facile contrasts between a sumptuous art which would be called Benedictine, and that denuded quality which was the special feature of Cistercian art. Monastic churches were usually of a limited size and sober style. This was especially the case with most of the houses which were dependent on Cluny. In each area, the architectural patterns were those in vogue during a given period. The exceptions were several basilicas which were centers for pilgrimages, such as Cluny and Saint-Benoit-sur-Loire, where proportions were adapted to other than monastic needs and the decor was occasionally of the same type as that of cathedrals and other secular churches. Since the Cistercians had desired strict solitude for all of their abbeys and prohibited general access to their churches, it was normal that these should be characterized by utmost simplicity. As the communities continued to grow, however, it became necessary to construct vast edifices, sometimes larger and no less costly than those of other monks. The buildings of the abbey of Fontenay, solid and impressive yet extremely well-proportioned, constructed according to St Bernard's specifications, bear witness to his awareness of architectural requirements. Bernard originated the monastery plans which spread from Clairvaux through various regions in Europe. Historians have spoken of a "Cistercian Plan," and the expression has been contested. But there surely was a plan which could be called "Claravallian," which is Bernardine. Perhaps what most reveals his esthetic sense are the manuscripts decorated by him. Here one recognizes masterpieces of pure calligraphy: an illumination that is plain, understated, sober in its color and lines, entirely at the service of writing which is elegant and carefully executed. For him, it was the writing that counted. No human image could add anything to this, but the splendor of the letters themselves commands respect. The great Bible of Clairvaux, today preserved at Troyes, is in the realm of painting what Fontenay is in the art of building: an example of the most balanced harmony between order and grace, between nobility of inspiration and poverty of means.

Was Bernard a musician? The question has been posed. He has given his name to a reform of Cistercian chant. But did he also offer technical advice? There is music in his style: he certainly "listened" to what he wrote. When he composed a liturgical office, that of St Victor for the Benedictine Abbey of Montieramey, he demonstrated his awareness of the rules of this particular literary genre. The meter of the hymns, the structure of the responses, the parody—that is paraphrase—in the antiphons, all reveal his familiarity with the tradition of this art form in the Church. Did he compose melodies? Nothing serves to affirm or deny it. Are the most astonishing things not to be expected from him? It would be difficult to imagine him refraining from personal intervention in the reform of the Cistercian chant which he endorsed by writing and signing the preface to the

Antiphonary. In any case, he believed full well in the effects
of melody on the heart and the mind. He wrote to the Abbot
of Montieramey:

> If there is chant, let it be very solemn, not harsh
> or wanton. Let it be pleasant, without being light,
> that it may charm the ear and thus move the
> heart. Let it alleviate sadness, let it calm anger.
> Let it not drain the text of its meaning, but make it
> fruitful.

And he continued to speak of the "spiritual grace" and the
realities to be attained by this kind of subtle innuendo—*in-
sinuandis rebus*—by cultivating this delight in sounds—*sic
mulceat aures*. Such a statement on the "fructification of the
letter" by beauty tells us much about Bernard's soul.

Was Bernard a philosopher? It has been stated and
denied. Certainly he was not in the ordinary sense of the
word. He even took precautions to insure that he would be
refused the title; he railed against others who bore it. But
with him, as with St Peter Damian, was this not merely a
literary theme? He observed and reflected: he was a
thinker. He had personal opinions on the subject of man, on
the union in man of reason and mortal flesh, on the functions
of the soul (animation, sensitivity, understanding), on its
"parts" (memory, reason and will), on its properties—
(reasonable, concupiscible and irascible). His particular
synthesis of these ideas is not elsewhere found. He
assimilated elements from different traditions, especially that
Socratic philosophy which placed such an emphasis on self-
knowledge. He used this date to serve his doctrine of the
image of God in man. He knew how to call on reason in his
teaching. Nevertheless, he was not a metaphysician of
genius like St Anselm, nor a dialectician like Roscelin. In this
sense, we can say that he was not a philosopher. But he did
have a philosophy, or at least there is some philosophy in his
works. It happens, however, that his rhetoric jeopardized his
logic. He was not resigned to writing as a professor; a certain need to charm, to allow for fantasy and an element of

surprise, sometimes prevented him from being very clear in his expression of abstract thought.

Bernard's Sources

Bernard was a man of the Bible. Was he an exegete? Yes, in the sense that he was constantly interpreting Scripture. But here again he applied himself to this task in a manner entirely his own. He had a precise, vast and profound knowledge of the sacred text. He had so woven it into the very fabric of his personal psychology that he made use of it, perhaps at times unawares, even when he did not quote it explicitly. His vocabulary is largely biblical. Phrases from the Latin Bible abound in his writing style, especially those of the four Gospels, St Paul (notably his Epistle to the Romans), the Psalms, and the Song of Songs. Many of his pages are simply mosaics of scriptural expressions, skillfully chosen, compared and arranged; one casting light on the other. And each word is usually employed with the same nuance that it has in its own context and situated in a whole where it will not seem discordant. Bernard did not compose a simple "chain" where texts were merely juxtaposed; he preferred the method of anthology, where extracts from assorted books are inserted into a well-constructed whole, like the Magnificat and other canticles found at the beginning of St Luke's Gospel. This familiarity with Sacred Scripture would lead us to believe that Bernard had done much reading in it. In fact, he could not have acquired this biblical sense without regular and frequent recourse to the Bible. However, we might ask, as paradoxical as it may seem, whether the Bible was for him primarily a book. He often quoted it, not according to the text that was prevalent at the time, the Vulgate, but according to the one which he found in the Fathers of the Church and especially in the liturgy. Evidently the chanted portions of the Divine Office, its responses and antiphons, were imprinted in his memory even more than were those of the Mass. He received his Scripture from tradition. For him, the Bible was the word of God living in the Church. It was part of a religious culture whose sources were inseparable, whose very mode of expression was harmonized into a unity.

He saw the Bible as an experience, as a means of participating in the redemption of the whole human race saved in Jesus Christ. God, in his love, spoke by the mouth of the prophets, then by his Incarnate Word, and finally through the Apostles. According to Bernard, inspiration is nothing but this personal intervention of God working in Christ and in the course of the history which prefigured him and transmitted his message. With this point of view, the interpreter's temptation is to project into the Old Testament the Christ who is revealed in the New, without taking sufficiently into account the gradual progression of God's work with his people. In this respect, Bernard's exegesis is sometimes too literal. Its merit lies in never losing sight of the evolutionary character of salvation. He was unaware of chronological data which we understand better today, but at least he was careful, when producing examples or arguments, to cite texts and facts in the order in which they succeeded each other. One of his favorite themes was the harmony between the two Testaments, and whenever the occasion presented itself, he demonstrated the transition from symbols to reality, from prophecies to realizations, from darkness to light. All is fulfilled in Christ and in the Spirit poured out on the Church. Bernard had no abstract conception of all of this, and for this reason it is difficult to extract from his writings any theory of inspiration. It is nevertheless possible, and we can see that for him inspiration did not differ from mystical experience, of which he had first-hand knowledge. There is certainly a danger of subjectivism in thus identifying personal charisms with those given for the entire Church and which she recognizes as authentic. At least we understand that, for Bernard, Sacred Scripture was not so much a subject of study as one of prayer. It is necessary to "taste", to "feel" how good God is. Bernard used this vocabulary of spiritual sensations with pleasure. For if the charity of God is at the origin of revelation, it must also be at its end point. All things tend toward love, and this supernatural sensitivity leads to willing surrender. The word of God encourages dialogue; it awaits the echo, the response which will be the word of man.

The true function of the poet in the Church is to make the words of God his own in order to make free use of them and to repeat them to God spontaneously. Bernard loved engaging in this sort of activity. His ways of handling biblical expressions varied: at one time he might exhaust every possible meaning of a word or else comment on the etymology; at another time he might group around a keyword, transformed into a major theme, other expressions which served to explain and enhance it; elsewhere he would change a letter or a syllable, replacing *claritas* with *caritas*; or pass from one word to a similar one, from *aemulemur* to *epulemur*, following the notion of charity with that of a feast. He would insert one biblical phrase into another, or modify a quotation in such a way that it was still recognizable. Occasionally, in order to provoke astonishment, he would indulge in deliberate misinterpretation, or he would place a verse in a different context from the one in which it originated, thus establishing a significance almost contrary to the original and obtaining an unexpected effect. All of this was artistically calculated: nothing was arbitrary. There was undoubtedly an element of contrivance, but this is in no way incompatible with spontaneity. We can often perceive the operation of what could be called a biblical psychology: a word, a sound calls from afar, awakens in the memory the phrase from which it was drawn and which will be cited in its own context farther on. But the use of this biblical language was carefully considered and consistent with specific requirements. Bernard combined biblical logic with a biblical rhetoric and poetry, very often with happy results. He excelled as well in other styles, but he gave his all in the biblical style. There he was most himself.

But how do we explain this need to "talk Bible"? Was this not merely a literary diversion? Are these not unworthy amusements when dealing with the words of God? Let us understand that, in the monastic culture of the Middle Ages, an encounter with Scripture was an encounter with Christ. Borrowing the language of the Bible was not a stylistic question; it was a means of prolonging the communion with Christ experienced while reading, hearing and praying the Sacred Scriptures. The biblical "word-game" does not signify a lack of interest in the true meaning of the words. It presupposes that this meaning is known as thoroughly as possible. It does not imply a stand outside or above Scripture, but rests within it. It does not deal with objective realities that are exterior to man, but speaks to the christian of the very thing by which he lives, of what is most intimate to him. In the process of reading, each member of the Church can verify within himself what is true of the whole redeemed people. Faith and fervor can discover more here than is revealed by historical and philological exegesis. They put us in touch with God. He it is whom we approach in and through Sacred Scripture; in His presence awakens an infinite respect for the words He has inspired, and a filial liberty toward the use which can be made of them. What is written to praise him becomes a new canticle, a poetical creation. The inner man exults, he is enraptured, and what he says is but a song of love inspired by the Spirit—*carmen Spiritus.*

Bernard's Bible was the one used by the Church in her ritual. In his style, liturgical recollections serve as inter-polations of Scriptural quotations. And where a mystery is celebrated by a particular feast or commemorated in the year of the Lord, it is always the liturgy that sets the tone and orients the interpretation. Thus, in Bernard's sermons, there is what could be called a "Biblical substratum"—a collection of scriptural texts which furnished the primary matter of the account, and a "liturgical background"—the mentality which created the atmosphere or the climate, and colored the whole. It is evident that, under such conditions, to translate a page of Bernard without losing this subtle flavor, these delicate nuances springing from biblical and liturgical Latin, is almost impossible. It would require the ability not only to render the ideas faithfully, but to awaken a thousand other resonances in

the ear and soul of the reader, assuming the reader would
already be familiar with the liturgy. Translation will always
impoverish Bernard's texts. The wonder of it is that, in spite
of all this, sufficient riches remain to please and to instruct.

The most comprehensive of Bernard's works is a kind of
"Liturgical Year", a long series of sermons in which he
commented on the mysteries of salvation and the texts which
proclaim them. Before his death, he gathered into this
collection all of the texts where he had previously explained
the feasts. In the case of each one, he revised, organized,
and, where necessary, completed in such a way as to make
each grouping equivalent to a treatise on Advent, Christmas,
Lent, Easter, and so on. But in this area also he demonstrated his creativity. He added to the heritage he received.
For example, with Advent: since the time of St Gregory the
Great, it had been customary to speak of two comings of
Christ—his coming to dwell among men in the Incarnation,
and his coming as judge at the time of the Parousia. Bernard
revealed another advent: his coming by grace to dwell in the
soul of the christian, which requires that the christian prepare
himself by purification. This third consideration may seem
obvious to us because we are accustomed to it, but it had to
be invented, that is, related to the Advent celebrated in the
liturgy. It was Bernard who accomplished this.

Finally, just as his Bible is liturgical, it is patristic. Not
only did he sometimes cite quotations according to a version
found in the Fathers of the Church which he had read or
heard in the Office, but he interpreted as they had taught
him. His exegesis is theirs. He was so imbued with their
way of thinking that he actually became one of them. He is
the most eminent representative of the "medieval patristics"
which doctrinal historians now admit truly existed. The latest
research, most notably that by Henri de Lubac, has
repeatedly identified points of similarity between Bernard and
Origen, St Augustine, St Ambrose, St Gregory of Nyssa, and
others, and has proven that these similarities cannot be
explained without acknowledging dependence. We know that
Bernard had a vast series of patristic writings reproduced for

his monastery at Clairvaux; a portion of these manuscripts is preserved at the Troyes Library. He used these for his reading and meditation. Moreover, in the course of conversation with someone like William of Champeaux, William of Saint Thierry, or some other master of the *sacra pagina*, his mental penetration permitted him to lay hold of an idea and to draw from it much more than had the one who first mentioned it. Bernard never repeats. He does not quote and he does not copy. He does not offer references, not because he wished to conceal his sources, but simply because he did not recall their existence. He pursued a thought which had become his own, and this makes it an extremely delicate affair to attempt an "investigation of his sources". Hardly ever is it possible to locate in an earlier author a formula or a teaching exactly like the ones we see in Bernard's writings. His oft declared intention was merely to bear witness to the doctrine of the Fathers. By the grace of God, he could not refrain from being himself. Though traditional, he is completely medieval. He experienced everything with the unique sensitivity of his age and expressed it in refreshing new language.

This is how he became the theologian and scholar revealed to us by the most recent investigations. In his work there is a "mystical theology" whose coherence and soundness Gilson had the merit to perceive more than thirty years ago. But there is also a dogmatic and moral theology, a doctrinal interpretation of the mysteries of God and of the christian condition. The notion of "theology as science" raises too many problems for us to make any worthwhile inquiry as to whether it applies to him. But we must at least emphasize that his teaching is not only of a practical nature, but includes as well a genuine theory of the relationship between man and God. In this sense, his theology has been justly classified as "speculative". All appearance of abstract learning, however, is covered over by the fact that he turned to the Bible, the liturgy and the Fathers of the Church as the sources and resources of his endeavors. His work is a reflection on christian revelation. From this point of view, Bernard cannot be distinguished from the other representatives, mostly monks and Canons Regular, of the traditional theology of his day. What he added to it was his experience. He trusted it as an authentic source and occasionally spoke of it as of the christian experience in general. He assumed it in his readers and referred them to it. He could do so legitimately because there is no knowledge of God without a corresponding life in God. But with him this experience took on forms and attained a degree proportionate to his natural talents and to his even greater gifts of grace. He was in a very real way—a very *realistic* way which we will try to specify farther on—a mystic. His teaching is marked by his experience: it is drawn from it and leads back to it. His doctrine is as it were suspended from moments of intense union with God, from summits of contemplative prayer. It participates in their exaltation and retains something of the mystery of these heights. We might sometimes wish that his theology on the nature of God and the Trinity, on the Creation of man, on the Angels, the Incarnation, salvation in Christ, the sacraments, the Church, death and eternal life, were clearer and more systematic, but we cannot deny its acuteness.

Bernard placed his talents as a stylist at the service of this intuitive thought. He was a writer and he knew it. He assumed the responsibilities and accepted the exigencies of the craft. The prefaces to his works and his literary correspondence reveal his concern for what has always been a psychological preoccupation of authors. He experienced that apprehension which the ancient orators called *trepidatio*, the trepidation of someone on the verge of risking his reputation and exposing himself to the judgment of his readers. He would apologize for writing, justify the fact by the requests he had received, and beg in advance the indulgence of critics. For each book he would state the title, the occasion and circumstances of its composition, the purpose of its publication, and the style adopted. He took care that each item produced conformed with the laws which governed it, and which were not the same for an epistle, a treatise or a sermon. To the first genre belong some five hundred letters on doctrine, friendship, or legal matters, of which two—collections circulated succesively during his lifetime—the second and more complete revised under his direction. One of these was a lengthy missive addressed to the Archbishop of Sens *On the Duties and Conduct of Bishops.* Geoffrey of Auxerre, in 1145, placed at the head of this collection a monastic manifesto which had already become legendary under the form of a letter sent to young Robert, Bernard's cousin, who had transferred from the novitiate of Clairvaux to Cluny.

Fairly early in his career, Bernard was asked to write down the oral teachings which he gave his monks. This was the origin of his first treatise, *On the Degrees of Humility and Pride.* Also dating from his early days as abbot were the four *Homilies in Praise of the Virgin Mary,* where he comments on the Gospel for the Annunciation. Shortly thereafter, around the year 1124, William of Saint Thierry obtained his intervention, by way of an *Apologia,* in the controversy on the subject of monastic observances which had set the Cistercians against the Cluniacs. To this same friend was later dedicated a small tract *On Grace and Free Will.* The Cardinal Chancellor of the Roman Church received a treatise *On the Love of God,* and the Grand Master of the Templars another *In Praise of the New Knighthood.* Then the monks of Saint-Pere de Chartres requested his advice *On Precept and Dispensation,* and Irish monks a *Life of Saint Malachy,* an Irish bishop who had died at Clairvaux during one of his voyages. Finally, under the title *On Consideration,* Bernard offered severe and sublime counsel to christianity's highest personnage, a former monk of Clairvaux who had become Pope Eugene III. Yet these occasional writings seem almost minor works compared to the great task begun in 1135 to which Bernard applied himself for eighteen years and left unfinished; a series of eighty-six *Sermons on the Song of Songs.*

Order and Beauty

Bernard's literary legacy is not vast. He wrote less than many others have done. His works have since been reproduced, printed and read in the West, always and everywhere. Proof of this lies in the innumerable manuscripts which have survived every occasion of loss and destruction, and the editions and translations that keep appearing. Why this kind of success? There is only one explanation: the quality of the work both in its inspiration and its expression. Bernard was a poet, an artist, a musician, a thinker: all of these talents are united in his style which reflects his intelligence and his good taste.

Bernard was a born writer. If we can believe Berengar, he had composed some verses already in his youth. And Geoffrey of Auxerre, at the beginning of Book Five of the "First Life", assures us that he wrote to the very end of his life: he was still dictating on his death bed. He seemed to take pleasure in trying his hand at such diverse literary genres as satire, descriptive portraits, the aphorism, the parable, the liturgical office, legends of hagiography, the epistle, the sermon, the treatise, and biblical commentary. Therefore his works should be read with consideration for the proper character of each one. His contemporaries did this more spontaneously than we since they were in closer contact with the literary traditions of antiquity. For example, the *Apologia* is not to be taken as an historical document that proposes to teach us about the Cluniac observances it denounces. It is a pamphlet destined to help its recipients by "reproving" them. It requires therefore a certain measure of irony and exaggeration. Humor can surpass the limits of good taste—not the case here—but it is legitimate and one should not be misled by it. When he developed the theme of an absurd meal, the Cluniac monks testing the wines and savoring elegant dishes (a theme used by others before him, but which he handled in a fresh and clever way) he was not pretending to describe actual menus. He was reminding the monks of the demands of monastic austerity by making them smile at themselves. In the many non-Cistercian monasteries which were taken to be models of this satirical masterpiece, there should have been gratitude toward the man who provided, at one and the same time, entertainment and a lesson in spirituality.

In what concrete fashion did Bernard write his works? He had secretaries and a chancellery mainly in charge of his less personal letters. For the rest, he was not satisfied to give directions. He dictated all of his texts word for word. This was especially true of the sermons which he had published. They were not delivered orally. If they include allusions to circumstances and to the listeners, it is because the particular genre required it. Bernard prepared himself for his written work, as he states at the beginning of his first sermon for All Saints Day. *Praeparavi.* And he compared this preliminary reflection to a light roasting in spiritual fire. In at least one case he said that he had first of all exchanged ideas in conversation, *conferendo,* with two other persons, one of whom was requested to write down the conclusions. Geoffrey of Auxerre likewise informs us that he would mark down on wax tablets the inspirations he received from God. Then came the moment of actual creation. He had first to project the ideas and words in a definitive manner, according to a plan conceived in advance. This involved two simultaneous operations which we are obliged to speak of in succession: the composition and the actual writing.

The first requirement for a literary work is arrangement of parts, the *dispositio* which was taught by the theorists and their given patterns. St Bernard explains: "Just as someone who writes conforms to certain rules, so the works of God conform to a specific order." Such an analogy accounts for both the precision and flexibility which characterize his art of composition. God's order is free, and Bernard's allows for fantasy. But even so, it is real. All of the methods taught by the rhetoricians and the authors of "Poetical Arts" he respected, beginning the piece with a general affirmation, then making transitions, apologies in the event of digression, returning to the original point, marking preference given to an artificial ordering, recalling what had been said previously, if useful, supplying a conclusion which summarized what had come before, and, if relevant, announcing the next sermon. Bernard did not ramble. He wrote, he composed. He knew how to vary his methods, but he did have methods. At one point, he will raise the circumstances which supply the answer to: Where? When? How? Why? and similar questions. At another, he will comment on the different prepositions which precede an object: *cum, in, a, pro, de, sub.* Elsewhere he abandons himself to a series of variations on prefixes determining the composition of derivations of the same word, as he does in Sermon 72 on the *Song of Song*, a kind of symphony on the history of God's efforts in man's behalf. He begins with the verb *spirare*, rises in crescendo from the day of Creation (*dies inspirans*) to that of glory toward which we tend (*dies adspirationis*), passing through the day of sin (*dies conspirans*), of spiritual death (*dies expirans*), of new life (*dies inspirans*), and of Paschal renewal (*dies respirans*). Each of these terms itself is surrounded by words which begin with the same prefix.

Many pages from St Bernard can be reduced to logical schemas, to synoptic tables, to two or three parallel columns where the ideas and sounds appear in exact correspondence. The entire *Consideration*, especially in Book V, is, from this point of view, truly a literary feat. The Thirty-ninth Sermon on the *Song of Songs*, referring to Pharaoh's cavalry, has this same quality: in six other passages, Bernard developed this same theme in a different way. Here he knew how to avoid the rigidity and redundance which could have resulted from an exposition of all of the elements of cautious symbolism. He left something to the creative imagination of the reader. It all happens as if Bernard saw in advance, in the form of a great tableau, the whole sermon or book, and the place that each idea, each phrase, and nearly every word would hold by a kind of formal necessity.

The second operation inherent in the act of writing is the editing. This also presupposes the utmost mental concentration. Each word chosen is at the same time precise, harmonious, and in accord with the context. Bernard's vocabulary is most often biblical and, according to the key text of each passage, he will depend on St Paul or St John or on the *Song of Songs* or on some other book. Occasionally it is speculative or juridical, but it always represents christian latinity and not secular. It bears besides a strong monastic imprint. To this fact of word-density must be added musical quality. The phraseology of a text destined to be read aloud is in large part a matter for the ear. Resonant effects are sought if they are not found spontaneously. Thus syllables beginning with the letter "v" abound when Bernard is praising the victory and virtue of St Victor. Elsewhere explosive consonants set the tone. Plays on words and sounds, alliterations, inflexions, rhymes, and verses contribute to the rhythm of every phrase and every page: whole paragraphs can be arranged in the form of free verse, with couplets, refrains, and repetitions. These many artifices are only revealed by very attentive reading. Bernard's texts are made to be not read, but analysed and studied. Some "number-plays" and cryptograms have even recently been discovered in his works, in places where the number of syllables reveals a word to which the text makes only a veiled allusion; or else where the length of the lines forms a figure symbolising the idea expressed by the phrases.

Thus the first sketch of a Bernardine writing was the result of a great art, but it did not satisfy the exacting requirements of its author. Bernard reread, listened anew, dictated corrections, and practised that *emendatio* recommended by the literary tradition. He modified mostly details: it was rare for him to rewrite a page or a sentence. But by changing a word, a syllable, or a letter—rather in the same way that we correct exams—he introduced new refinements into an already perfect prose. The variant readings of the successive and authentic collections of his works as they are preserved in manuscript form allow us to witness the author's labors and appreciate the improvements he made in his style. During the last five years of his life, this elderly abbot, who was also a very active man of the Church, took pains to review his own major works, letter by letter, in order to prepare a revised edition. He intended to leave to posterity writings whose beauty would be worthy of the mysteries of God.

We should be able to illustrate by example the findings

summarized here. More and more, St Bernard appears as a master of the written word. He knew the rules of the art and he complied. He had models and he drew inspirations from them. But he freed himself from both in an inspired fashion. His prose is a poetical transposition of traditional rhetorical methods. He was a poet, and all the riches of his soul were at the service of his inspiration. For example, with vivid imagination he pictured Pharaoh, his chariots, his horsemen, his satraps, their mounts and their equipment, the detailed account of their trappings with fans, baldachins and the whole sumptuous retinue of an oriental prince! The intensity of his emotion and the force of his intelligence are no less significant. There were resources in him which could become formidable when he applied himself to invective, but which usually gave him tremendous powers of persuasion and even of seduction. Both he and his contemporaries were aware of this: John of Salisbury and others bear witness to it. In all works, he admitted his own weaknesses, defects in style, shortcomings in composition. But they are nearly always a success. He had complete mastery over his talent, checked his fluency, subdued and ordered the images, words and ideas which crowded into his mind at the moment of writing, at the moment of that liberating tension which he describes so well in Letter 89:

> What mental turmoil for those who dictate! The reververations of a multitude of formulas, a variety of phrases, diversity of meanings; it is often necessary to discard what is present, to seek out what has been overlooked, to pay close attention to what will be the most beautiful expression, the most logical from the point of view of the senses, the clearest for the mind, the most useful for the reader's conscience; finally, to take care in placing each part before or after another, and to think of many other points observed by those who are learned in the matter.

The result of all of this interior labor is that well-balanced and austere prose, like the illuminations of Clairvaux and the architecture of Fontenay, whose total quality is not easy to grasp at first reading. Bernard is a difficult and delightful author. He encourages effort and, at times, he is discouraging; but more often he enlightens and comforts. Many who do not suspect the subtleties contained therein— and which he no doubt made a point to conceal—appreciate this blending of sobriety, almost a classicism, with a poetical and resonant charm. Traditional and patristic, Bernard is at the same time completely medieval. He was already modern or, more precisely, he is a man for all seasons, because he satisfies what is most universal in man: the need to rise above himself, to be in communion with a beauty which surpasses him.

BERNARD'S INFLUENCE

His Sons

BERNARD WAS REALLY A MONK for only two years. He was a novice in preparation for being a monk, and two years after his profession he became abbot of Clairvaux and remained in office for thirty-eight years. His entire work was determined by this office which he had received from God in his Church, and to whose exercise he gave himself totally. He was frequently absent from his monastery, in a measure which seems to represent approximately one third of his time. But he always returned to Clairvaux: it was there that he most often lived, from there that he judged many matters, and it was always from this viewpoint that he made his decisions. The most recent investigations show him to have been practically obsessed with developing and extending his monastery. The life lived there seemed to him so close to the ideal program for all christian existence that he unceasingly referred to it. He welcomed those whom God sent, attended to their formation and government, and then, with them, he founded new Clairvaux. The first problem which poses itself in this respect is the exceptional recruitment of this monastery. There is nothing abnormal in the fact that Bernard received everyone who presented himself. But did he not also attract, indeed monopolize and lay claim to, others with an insistence and even an indiscretion which were not altogether disinterested? It cannot be denied. For example, his attitude toward Phillip of Harvengt, prior of the monastery of Canons Regular of Bonne-Esperance, on the subject of a religious from this community who had gone to Clairvaux without his superior's consent, is not above reproach. There were other cases where, in order to appease his own desire to see many christians, even those already committed to some other group, serving God in his community, Bernard made use of his influence and prestige—which were difficult to resist, as he well knew. Not only did he act this way with regard to religious of other observances, but it seems that he likewise evidenced a certain exclusivism within the Cistercian Order itself in favor of the filiation of Clairvaux: other Cistercian lines, especially that of Morimund, seemed to have sensed this. Such are the facts. In order to understand and perhaps excuse them, we must recall his idea of the christian vocation. He revealed it in many texts, but especially in that treatise in the form of a sermon, *On Conversion*, where he demonstrated his penetrating analysis of the conditions of the soul.

According to him, every christian hears the voice of God calling him interiorly to leave aside his sin and strive toward a love which will open the ways of prayer. This vocation assumes an evolutionary and dynamic character: it is constant and stimulates a continuing progress. To have responded once for all is not enough. It requires a sustained and growing fidelity. It can be realized in two ways: in the world or in the cloister. Clerics and laymen are the fist case. More than is sometimes apparent, Bernard admitted that they could sanctify themselves in the world. They practice love of God and neighbor, the latter manifesting itself mostly through exterior and corporal works of mercy. One can be saved without following the evangelical counsels, but there is no salvation without love. For clerics also, salvation is possible in the world but difficult. The proof of their love of God and neighbor is their zeal in the service of souls, which constitutes the spiritual work of mercy proper to their state. There is no pastoral life without charity. Where then will be the surest guarantee of this charity? Bernard replies: in the cloister. The monastic vocation is the best means of satisfying the double exigency which grace places in the heart of every christian: personal purification and communion in the life of the whole Church. The christian vocation is this "law" of God working in the soul and stimulating the will to seek out that state of life most favorable to its growth. The monastic vocation is a particular but privileged realization of this universal vocation. Those who hear the call to the cloister thus have an obligation to obey and to persevere in order to make progress. So, between entrance into the Church by Baptism and entrance into heaven by way of death, many paths are open: the most certain is also the most narrow.

As for the institutions which regulate the states of life, they are necessary and should normally be respected. They remain subordinate however to the spiritual development of individuals. This sense of the variety of charisms explains in large part Bernard's attitude toward religious who wished to change observance, usually in order to enter Clairvaux. In several cases, he discouraged them in advance or, if they did come, sent them back home. Sometimes he called to mind the principles of tradition and the law in force which little favored such *transitus*. In actual practice, when the subjects insisted, he consented to receive them, not wishing to oppose what he called the *libertas Spiritus*, the freedom of the Holy Spirit operating in the soul of the man. He says in Letter 84: "Often the attempt to lead a more austere life has a soothing effect on anxious souls for whom the state to which they have been committed was not sufficient." If they persevered in their new way of life, it was proof that they were following their vocation, whose demands they had but gradually come to perceive. Institutions should remain flexible enough to allow for this growing quest of the absolute God. And soon after St Bernard's time and under his influence, canonical legislation relative to transfers from one observance to another was relaxed in a definitive way throughout the Church.

Monastic Formation

How did Bernard form his novices and teach his monks?

His writings can enlighten us on his teaching, but not on the manner in which he delivered it. He undoubtedly spoke of the same realities—the christian mysteries, the requirements of charity—which occupied his thoughts when he drew up his written works in a style so refined that he could not have improvised it. His listeners could not have appreciated it nor, in many cases, even have understood it. He had an extremely precise conception of monastic obligations, especially of obedience, the occasion and proof of charity. The monks made profession and promised obedience according to "the Rule of St Benedict", and the first words of this formula, *secundum Regulam*, excluded everything that would be opposed (*contra*), outside of (*praeter*), beyond (*ultra*), or short of (*citra*) the prescriptions of the text. In accepting this promise which the monks make in his presence and to which he is witness and guarantor, the abbot it committed to observe the Rule himself and to see that it is observed by others. He cannot dispense from obligations fixed in the Rule. The limits of authority are determined by the Rule which puts the demands of the Gospel in concrete terms for the monks. Bernard devoted several epistles and the treatise *On Precept and Dispensation* to subtle problems of this nature.

But to recommend this doctrine daily to ordinary monks, we find great simplicity of language in this extraordinary abbot! We have as proof numerous texts which he took care not to publish, but of which his listeners preserved the general scheme, and sometimes even the written version, which is very different from those solemn works he destined for publication. His imagination was given free rein; he invented stories and parables, set characters in a scene and recounted their dialogue. One day he compared the characteristics of monastic life to the fourteen properties of the dental system. Another time, he described in great detail the procession of heavenly choirs receiving the Lord at the time of his Ascension. On another occasion, he developed the theme of the seven words spoken by Mary. Or else he lingered on the symbolism of the seven baths of Naaman. Of these picturesque discourses there remains but a sober mention in the published sermons. But how lively the "sentences" or "brief sermons" are, reports written by some of his disciples, which have transmitted the complete or summarized text of these familiar conferences. We can well understand the charming impression left by his preaching. *Quam iucunda*, as Geoffrey of Auxerre would later say. And he would insist on this joyous and even playful devotion, *iucunda devotio*, of which Bernard himself had spoken more than once in his writings.

Government

He taught with a great deal of human feeling: *humano quodam more*—once again words from Geoffrey of Auxerre. He governed in the same way. Otherwise there could be no explanation for the fact that hundreds of men came to live with him, persevered, and then allowed themselves to be sent off on distant foundations. One single example here will conjure up the daily life of Clairvaux. It does not require commentary. It should demonstrate all the human weakness that remained in Bernard as well as the greatness of his humility, his obedience to the Rule, and his charity toward all. He wrote to the Abbot of Trois-Fontaines in Letter 70:

> By way of example, I will tell you about something similar that once happened to me. It was when my brother Bartholomew was still alive. One day he displeased me. Trembling with rage and using a threatening expression and tone of voice, I ordered him to leave the monastery. He immediately walked out, went to one of our barns, and stayed there. When I learned of this I wanted to call him back, but he stated his conditions: he would only return if he were received in his own rank; not in the last rank and as a fugitive, but as if he had been sent away lightly and without just cause. He maintained that he should not have to submit to due process of the Rule for his return,

since proper procedures had not been observed in his dismissal. Distrusting my own judgment of this response and of my own actions, and because of the ties of blood between him and me, I entrusted the decision of this affair to the hands of all the brethren. Thus they judged, in my absence, that his return should not be subject to the letter of the Rule since it was certain that his dismissal had not been conducted in a regular fashion.

This text was taken from one of the exhortations to forgiveness contained in Bernard's correspondence. In twelve of his Letters (55, 70, 84, 86, 101, 102, 297, 399, 400, 414, 417, 445), he intervened in favor of religious who had left their monastery under one pretext or another, most often by reason of their own instability. The "fugitives", as they were called, were numerous at that time. When they returned, as they nearly all did, it was sometimes difficult to have themselves received again. Monks of different orders had recourse to Bernard and he interceded for them. For example, he writes at the end of Letter 414 to the monk Alard who had expelled a novice:

Thus I beg you, what this brother could not obtain from you by his own prayers, may he at least obtain it by our own since he came so far in search of them.

Bernard excelled in this art of letters of recommendation, consolation, or reconciliation.

Nuns

There can be no question here of mentioning everything, but, among the numerous aspects of his monastic activity, there is one which cannot be omitted because of what it reveals to us of Bernard's soul: his concern for nuns. He took it upon himself to secure the material resources they needed. He signed as witness several acts—no doubt also instigated by him—which conferred donations and guaranteed

protection for or confirmed their estates. And this on behalf
of houses of different observances: Benedictines at Jully
where he sent his sister Humbelina who later became
prioress, or at Pralon, Larrey, Puits-d'Orbe, Yerres; Fonte-
vrists whose defense he assumed when a quarrel opposed
them to the Bishop of Angers; Cistercians at Le Tart and its
daughter houses, and others who were independent. He
seems to have compelled the Benedictines of Poulangy (where
his niece Adeline had entered) to adopt Cistercian customs,
from which they soon freed themselves. To these communities and others he directed postulants, sometimes very great
ladies whom he had persuaded to convert during the course
of his travels. He also knew how to make them take precautions against themselves. For Jully, in accord with the
Abbot Hugh of Pontigny, he counseled the promulgation of
very strict rules of cloister. Was this really necessary? In a
letter to the Archbishop of Trier, he denounced the grave
abuses evident among the nuns of Saint Maur in Verdun; and
he did so with that rhetorical style inspired by Scripture
which he used in all his writings and which makes it difficult
to know exactly what the situation was. The letter which
Abelard addressed to him early in their friendship preserves
the memory of one of Bernard's visits to the Paraclete:

> The abbess, who is your daughter in Christ and
> our sister, has told me with the utmost joy that,
> after they had so long desired your presence, you
> came to see them; and that, in the manner of an
> angel rather than a man, you comforted her as
> well as her sisters by your saintly exhortations.

Abelard also used rhetoric, but we can imagine the
impression made by the bearing and the words of this extraordinary man, everywhere so long awaited: *diu desideratum.*
He observed. In this case, he noted certain innovations
introduced into the liturgy by Abelard. Abelard felt obliged
to offer an explanation, which is how we know of the incident.
But surely in many other cases, unknown to us, Bernard
offered the communities of nuns where he had guided his

daughters the joy of an occasional chat!   Moreover, he remained devoted to Heloise even long after Abelard's death. It seems that he paid her other visits, and in his Letter 270, which dates from his later years, he recommended her to Pope Eugene III.

Human Relationships

Bernard's activities extended outside his cloister, into other cloisters, and then into the world, in ever-widening circles for which Clairvaux remained the center.   He intervened in the public affairs of the Church, but he could not have been so effective had it not been for the personal relationships which he had established with so many men and women in society. It is impossible to understand his influence without trying to situate it in relation to the causes which he served, both those of a private nature and those which were universal.   The richness of his character helped him.   He possessed an intense capacity for getting on well with others.   Some of his friendships are well known, for example, those which bound him to William of Saint Thierry, to Malachy O'Morghair, or to Aelred of Rievaulx, whom he urged to write a book entitled *The Mirror of Charity*.   His friendship with Peter the Venerable has been placed in doubt because of the great part played by rhetoric in the letters they exchanged.   But literature does not explain everything and, with Bernard, once we get beyond the formulas of courtesy, the tone is unmistakable.   He also had a great number of more obscure friends.

In his correspondence, the vocabulary of friendship is abundant, varied, precise, and exceptionally consistent, and it expresses an idea, even more a doctrine which is one of his most coherent.   Charity engenders friendships: she is a mother, as he says in Letter 11.   She is a gift from God, comes from him and leads back to him, but she works through human emotions which she transforms and elevates without suppressing them.   St Bernard goes on: "Because we are carnal, our desire and our love must begin with the flesh.'' (Letter 11)   In Letter 116, he stated that God inscribes in our hearts a love toward our friends which they cannot read, but which we can reveal to them.   There results what he calls an *affection* [*affectio*] and even more often, an *affectus*, a profound and ineffable attachment of an experiential order which determines the rules and obligations of friendship.   It can advise, exhort, make known its needs; above all it can offer joyful encouragements.   It suffers from prolonged separation and desires to see the loved one over and over again, even for short periods of time if it can be more often.

We could quote many ardent and tender formulas, filled with human feeling.   Consider, for example, the pleasure caused by a letter:

> I glanced through your letter for a brief moment, but with great affection.   I am so busy... But I have withdrawn, broken away from the requests and rejoinders of all; I have locked myself in with my secretary Nicholas, whom you also love. I have read and reread the great sweetness which emanated from your letter.   (Letter 389)

And, on another occasion:

> Your letter has reached me at a very busy time... I barely had time to read it at table, for it was just then given to me.   And it is only with difficulty that I can stealthily encroach on my schedule to send you these few words....   (Letter 88)

He wanted the latest news; he worried:

> As your dear Ovid would say: 'How many times have I feared dangers more terrible than true.' Anxious about everything because I am not informed, I often prolong a real sadness over imaginary woes.   In fact, a heart once truly seized by love is no longer at its own disposal.   (Letter 74)

He consoled the Archbishop of Rouen who was having trouble with the people of his diocese; the Abbot of Foigny who was overcome by the burdens of office; the parents of Geoffrey of Peronne who were grieved by the entrance of their son into Clairvaux: "We adopt him as a brother and we adopt you as parents.... I will be his father, his mother, his brother, his sister." (Letter 110) He congratulated old Bishop Atto of Troyes who had recovered his health. He spoke also of his own and others' health, without humor, and certainly without any illusions about remedies:

> The Archbishop of Lyons stayed for some time at Montpellier; there he spent on medicines all that he had, as well as what he did not have. (Letter 307)

This big-hearted man, this father of so many monks, concerned himself with laymen, and he gave good reason:

> In every place we are at the service of the same Lord, we fight under the same King: the same grace from God has its worth in the public forum and in the cloister. [*Et in foro et in claustro gratia Dei eadem valet*] (Letter 490)

Clerics and laymen he believed necessary for the security of the City of God, of the Spouse. they are one reality, the Church—*Unum sunt.* (*On the Song of Songs,* 76, 8) But among them exist different states, *ordines.* There are virgins and consecrated souls, widows and spouses. On several occasions, and especially against the Cathari, Bernard affirmed the dignity and sanctifying value of marriage. He addressed himself more than once to great men, to the Emperor, to kings and princes, to those men of the lesser nobility whose milieu was familiar to him since he had noble origins himself. With urbanity, using a courtly style but soon by-passing it in order to let his heart speak, he often gave evidence of a freedom of speech not lacking in courage. He had little understanding for the efforts of the bourgeoisie at Rome or at Reims to obtain freedom. To those of Toulouse,

Pisa, Milan, he simply recommended works of mercy. For those at Genoa, he insisted on patience and perseverance in doing good, which would assure interior harmony and condition exterior peace. He tended to identify civic prosperity with the political interests of the papacy. At a moment when communes, especially in Italy and France, were obtaining or winning their freedom, he remained a stranger to the movement and represented a conservative tendency. He dealt only with religious problems. He was anxious to have men of all categories, even the anti-social, working for the causes of the Church, and he rejoiced to see enrolled in the army of the Crusades "murderers, thieves, adulterers, perjurors and all other criminals." Finally, Geoffrey of Auxerre, who had often accompanied him on his voyages, stated in a sermon which he delivered on the anniversary of Bernard's death that he was still moved by the memory of the way in which Bernard counselled

> ...the peasants and the women of the common people to help one another. He taught them to lend bread to their neighbors with a smile, to invite to their own meal a neighbor who had been too busy to prepare food, or to bring him vegetables to offer him small dishes (*exigua communicare pulmenta*).

This man knew how to meet everyone at his own level.

About fifteen of his letters are addressed to women, and their names sound like characters from a novel: Beatrice, Melisand, Sophie, Mathilda, Adelaide, Adeline, Ermengarde. He was not afraid to indulge in effusions whose style at first seems somewhat affected, even pedantic, but later becomes spontaneous and ardent. For example, he writes to the Countess Ermengarde of Brittany:

> Would to God that you could read my heart as you do this letter. You would see what a profound love for you has been engraved there by the Finger of God... My heart is near you, even if I am absent in body.... (Letter 116)

And on another occasion:

> My heart overflows with joy when I learn that your
> own is at peace. Your joy is mine, and the bright-
> ness of your gaiety is health for my soul... Truly I
> begrudge the business which prevents me from
> going to see you... It is true that I cannot often do
> so but, rare as it may be, it offers me that much
> greater happiness.... (Letter 117)

He was sensitive to the attentions, the signs of concern
which came to him from women. He asked of Beatrice:

> What relative, what friend looks after me as you
> do? Who worries about my health as you do?...
> All look upon me as a man who is no more: only
> you cannot forget me. (Letter 118)

To Mathilda, the Countess of Blois, who had complained of
her son's instability, he counselled indulgence toward the
young man: "A son can occasionally forget that he is a son,
but a mother cannot and should not forget that she is a
mother." And he added, with a bit of psychology: "To
reprimand and reproach him would only serve to exasperate
him further." (Letter 300) After having prayed over the
difficult birth of Prince Henry, he took the liberty to write to
another Mathilda, the Queen of England:

> Take the greatest care of that son whom you have
> just brought into the world; let me say, without
> offense to the king, your spouse, that I am also, to
> a certain extent, his father.

These pretty speeches, which are almost a kind of flattery,
gave him the right to beg—and he made use of it. He wrote
to the Count of Champagne, the spouse of the Countess
Mathilda:

> As I was passing through Bar recently, a poor
> beggar woman, full of grief, sought me out. The
> account of her sorrows distressed me.... It is the
> wife of that Belin whom you had to punish

severely some time ago because of his crime.
Please have pity on this woman, and God will also
have pity on you. (Letter 39)

It is nice to know that in the life of this delightful man, who
was quite a charmer, feminine friendship and concern for
common people were not missing.

THE MAN OF ACTION

Public Affairs

IN BERNARD, a man rich in natural gifts and a humanist in his talents, the art of persuasion and personal charm created a formidable capacity for power. His ability to convince, and sometimes even to seduce, opened to him possibilities in the realm of government which came with some little risk. Could he escape the temptation to power? He recognized its value. He was esteemed on all sides: he was called upon and agreed—sometimes even taking the initiative himself—to launch himself into public affairs. We cannot enumerate here everything in which he was involved, for this would amount to tracing the religious-political events in the West over a period of thirty years. At least the principal aspects of this activity can be mentioned. In all areas where it was exercised, Bernard intervened with certain constant dispositions, determined by the ideas of his time—which we must take care not to judge according to our own—and by what he himself was: a vigorous personality in whom it is difficult to distinguish—as it undoubtedly was for him also—what comes by nature and what by grace.

To what extent did he have the right or the duty, as a man of the Church, to take part in affairs of state? Would he not have been well advised to abstain from the political game, where passions, self-interest and the fascination of power cause such trouble? Did this not become a threat to the purity of his union with God and his fidelity to his monastic

51

vocation? On the other hand, should he not have attempted to foster respect for God's demands? In different milieux, many if not all his contemporaries considered him the master of the hour: the monasteries needed him, in his own Order and in traditional monasticism where William of Saint Thierry and the religious of Saint-Père of Chartres had recourse to him; the hierarchical Church consulted him and Rome accepted his advice on the episcopal elections in France, England and elsewhere; princes and knights turned to him for direction. He found himself involved in national and international conflicts. Cities in Italy, Aquitaine, Flanders and the Rhineland acclaimed him. He had withdrawn from the world, and the expansion of the Cistercian Order, particularly the line of Clairvaux, offered him both the occasion and means to animate a vast reform movement. Through his communication with all of these houses, he was in contact with all of the nerve centers of christianity: couriers were continually delivering his messages and returning with information and requests.

Thus his life always included participation in both contemplation and action, an alternation of one and the other, and this kind of dialectic is reflected in his writings. Business letters and controversial works and events of the moment were succeeded by biblical and liturgical commentaries and mystical accounts. In the very year of his death, the Archbishop of Trier called him to Lorraine to mitigate a conflict between the Duke of Lorraine and the Bishop of Metz, and Bernard, on his return, continued to dictate the *Sermons on the Song of Songs*.

In his soul was a continual temptation to power. He endeavored to overcome it by means of humility, love, and the will to serve. But the fact remains, and is not even doubtful, that he occasionally succumbed to some extent, if only in using too readily his powers of influence. At such times, God intervened to purify him through defeat. If Bernard knew success, he also felt the resistance of men; even those who were most indebted to him and whom he had served well, Innocent II and Eugene III, did not stand by him to the end.

The attempt at a Crusade which he had launched proved a failure, and he felt and accepted the humiliation. His soul shared in both success and disappointment. Others would have been discouraged by this suffering, which resulted from lack of understanding on the part of some, and occasionally those in the highest places, while at the same time the greater number were listening to him. But he remained confident because his hope was in the God whom he willed to serve. He continued to speak with assurance, advising, threatening, finding fault, like an untiring prophet. He went very far in his use of authority. In order to impose what he believed to be the will of God, he sometimes imposed his own. Nevertheless, as we saw in his advice to religious transfering from one observance to another, he respected the mystery of souls. He wrote about freedom because he truly believed in it. He was a fighter, and he preached peace. His conduct occasionally seemed to accord ill with his doctrine. It is to the doctrine that he eventually turned for the resolution of these apparent antinomies. If there can be doubt concerning the worth of the means which he employed, there can be no hesitation as to his intentions or his absolute faith in Christ. Let us attempt to recall his activities.

Political Life

First of all, there was the entire range of political life. It was certainly a matter of religious politics, but it was not less dangerous for that. And by what right did Bernard intervene? Like almost all of his contemporaries, he shared the conviction which Gregory VII did so much to propagate: that, even if the temporal and spiritual are distinct, they cannot be separated. But the spiritual is superior and has the responsibility of guiding the temporal to its end, which is the same as that of all human endeavors: the fulfillment of God's Will. Nevertheless, Bernard differed from Gregory VII in that he tended to limit the role of papal power in the temporal sphere; not that he excluded it, but, in the realization of this collaboration between the two powers, he believed less in institutions than in personal integrity. He laid more stress on personal merit and sanctity than on authority. Thus in the texts where he approaches this problem there are apparently contradictory statements. On the whole, his conception can be summarized in this celebrated formula from *On Consideration:*

> Both swords, the material and the spiritual, belong to the Church: but one is drawn by the Church and the other for the Church; one by the hand of the priest, the other by that of the knight, but at the request of the priest and by order of the Emperor.

Clear expressions, but their application was not precise, and they could give rise to many interpretations.

How did Bernard in fact behave? He devoted himself to moral action, achieving an exercise of power only indirectly and concentrating on the formation of individuals. He offered good advice to princes on the subject of government. He insisted on justice as a requirement of charity. In coercion or in punishment, one cannot be just without mercy; in the administration of material goods, one cannot save his own soul without taking an interest in others, especially the common people. Bernard wrote some forceful pages on property as a social charge. In particular, he demonstrated that luxury is a form of injustice since the money which it costs should be spent on behalf of the poor. He addressed to laymen the same protests against ostentation which he raised in *On the Duties and Conduct of Bishops.* To all those who held power, at whatever level of society, he also preached peace. He thundered against private wars, to useless and fatal tournaments which often led to more serious strife, even to conflict between entire regions. In his treatise *In Praise of the New Knighthood,* he was hard on the knighthood of his time. He tried to prevent or stop local wars, launched from motives of prestige, vengeance or conquest. In Letter 97 to Duke Conrad of Zeringen, he proposed sending several religious from his monastery to obtain a truce between the Duke and Count Amedeas of Geneva. In conflicts between powerful princes, he encouraged recourse to negotiation rather than war. In 1142, he interceded with Innocent II to obtain peace between King Louis VII of France and Count Thibaut of Champagne. And in a personal letter to the King, he acknowledged his role as Jonas calling the King of Ninevah to repentance. This was the nature of Bernard's interventions: he was a prophet who spoke on the part of God to the conscience of men. He believed less in institutions than in virtue. There is no evidence that he was involved in the functioning of those institutions of peace which existed during his time. But he exhorted and threatened. He begged, and often he obtained.

Religious Politics

In the area of religious politics, he acted in the same way. His doctrinal works propose a moral program for the prelate. In his *Life of Saint Malachy* he illustrated this ideal by the example of a reformed and reformer bishop, as Bernard conceived him. In practice, he tried to have positions filled by men who had been won over to these ideas. They were often monks and came from Clairvaux or houses of that filiation. According to him, the ecclesiastical reform needed to depend on the monastic reform and draw inspiration from same. Bernard conceived of the Church rather in the image of his community, which occasionally blinded him to certain aspects present in all complex situations. He plunged impetuously into an activity which ended in the triumph of his own candidates, without any sign of that disinterestedness which would have been expected of him. He had his closest collaborator, the prior of Clairvaux, named to the See at Langres so that this monastery could avoid having as its bishop a monk from Cluny. He managed to put forth another monk from Clairvaux, Henry Murdach, for the Archbishopric of York because the abbots of Clairvaux' foundations in this region opposed the candidate of the British Crown, William Fitzherbert, who regained the See after Murdach's death and eventually was canonized. In these affairs and in similar ones, Bernard acted on faith, according to information

received but not always checked, or under the persuasion that
the interests of the churches and the Church were identical
with his own ideas on the subject.   And since he was
Bernard, he prevailed.   But at what price God alone can
judge.

With regard to the papacy, he did not remain inactive. He
was stimulated by the fact that he knew himself to be a
subject of debate in the Roman court.   He had to overcome
this resistance.   On the one hand, the Apostolic See owed
him a great deal; on the other hand, the very pontiffs whom
he had helped, as well as members of their entourage, feared
his influence—which they had not hesitated to call upon when
necessary.   This state of affairs began as early as the year
1130.   Bernard was only forty years old at the time.   A double
election had raised to the pontifical throne the representatives
of two factions which divided the clergy and the people of
Rome, Innocent II and Anacletus II.   Bernard, once again
inclined to consider personal merit, disinterestedness, and
tendencies toward reform rather than to judge the proper
functioning of the institutions, immediately took Innocent's
part.   He exerted himself to obtain in his behalf the appro-
bation of Louis VI of France and Henry I of England.   In the
service of this cause, he traveled through parts of France and
Germany and three times went to Italy, winning over Pisa
and Genoa in 1133, Milan in 1135, and attempting to obtain
the approval of Roger II of Sicily in 1137.   No sooner had that
victory been won than another struggle began between the
Roman Senate and Pope Lucius II.   Arnold of Brescia would
protest to the papacy not much later against the wealth of the
clergy in away reminiscent of Bernard's attitude.   But the
Abbot of Clairvaux invited reform not revolution, and he
became Arnaud's adversary.   Then in 1145 he found himself
more closely associated with the government of the Church
than ever.   One of his sons, a monk from Clairvaux, became
Pope under the name Eugene III.   What occasions and
temptations to power this presented for Bernard!

He soon wrote to Eugene III: "It is said that you are not
the Pope but in fact I am: great numbers of those who have

affairs in court come to me from all sides." (Letter 239) Aided by his chancellory, he devoted himself to the task. Clairvaux became like a branch of Rome, and more in high places saw it as a rival. Innocent II and Eugene III preserved their autonomy; they were exposed to the influence exercised both by Bernard's admirers and by his enemies. They seemed to be surrounded by a whole group of cardinals and Curia members who came largely from monastic circles or from the Canons Regular of France and the Rhineland, partisans of Bernard, of his ideas on the reform of the Church, and of the causes which he defended. But there also existed a "Roman" tendency jealously attached to the prerogatives of the Curia and its independence from the Abbot who stirred such commotion from Clairvaux. The popes sought to retain their freedom of decision. Bernard was kept informed of all of these stirrings of passion. Occasions continued to arise when he had to exercise his influence and make use of his contacts. From such a distance, how could he make judgments and dominate such complex and varied situations while still remaining the abbot, the friend, the writer that we know? It was in the realm of doctrinal conflicts that he ran his greatest risks.

Doctrinal Conflicts

It was easy enough for Bernard to reinforce the traditional faith when it was challenged by the "popular heresies." He did so in his *Sermons on the Song of Songs* 63-66, at the request of Eberwin of Steinfeld, who was concerned about the errors of the Cathari in the region of Cologne. At about the same time, in 1145, Bernard himself went to refute other Cathari in Languedoc, and particularly the disciples of the monk Henry who rejected the ecclesiastical hierarchy and referred to a purely spiritual Church which had not only nothing of the carnal in it, but nothing related to the senses. It was likewise easy for Bernard, in his lengthy Letter 77, to respond to questions posed to him by Hugh of Saint Victor on the subject of the necessity of Baptism or other minor questions of theology. But the situation grew worse when it came to confronting an adversary as original in his problems and methods and as vigorous in his thinking as Abelard. This confrontation in fact occurred in 1139 and 1140, under complex and painful circumstances, many elements of which have eluded historians. The chronology of texts and facts is still disputed. One part of the documentary dossier containing some of Abelard's writings is either unpublished or lost. In the presence of the powerful and admired master of the Schools, Bernard, the simple abbot of Clairvaux, has been compared to David in the face of Goliath. Undoubtedly he acted with courage. But did he perhaps use weapons forbidden in an honest contest between equals?

Here we must distinguish two areas, the doctrines debated and the procedures employed in the controversy. As for the former, there is now a unanimity among historians acknowledging the worth of the points of view defended by each of the two protagonists. Bernard never set himself up against dialectic as such nor against arguments of reason. He himself occasionally made use of them in his writings. On the other hand, Abelard was not a heretic. His own intention was to defeat the dialecticians, enemies of the faith, on their own territory. Part of his teaching touched on problems of logic, particularly on the unity of the universal, that is, of an essence which remains the same in its diverse individual manifestations—the famous "quarrel on universals." Other points were directly concerned with the interpretation of christian doctrine: what should be given to the intellect and what to authority? What method should consequently be adopted in theology? How should the substantial union in Jesus Christ of human nature and the Word be understood? What is the relationship between the Person of Christ and the second Person of the Trinity? Was the Redemption satisfaction of a juridical order or a work of love? In the area of sin, is intention not more important than the act itself? These are delicate problems, and, for their solution, the proper use of the language of logic was as important as it was difficult. On none of these points did Abelard intend to shatter the faith of the Church, to play the role of "active adversary of Catholic dogma,'' as he is now glorified by certain propagandists in Eastern Europe. At the most he could have committed an ''error in the faith'' or been the occasion of such error among some of his disciples because of the conclusions that he reached on certain particular points by means of argumentation conducted according to a method which was in itself legitimate. In a new way and with an unprecedented penetration, Abelard considered all the problems concerning God, Redemption, the faith, grace, sin, moral conscience; he set the pace for decisive progress in theology. At the same time, and because of the very novelty of his views, he used formulas which were inaccurate or inexact. To students less intelligent than himself, he furnished a pretext for expressions wide open to criticism. Thus there *was* matter for discussion. The question is to discover whether it was conducted as it should have been.

Each of the two adversaries was a man, had admirers and disciples, and had at his disposal means of influence. Bernard had personal charm, his spiritual radiance; Abelard had his powers of reasoning. Each one used the weapons he had. The misfortune was that these weapons were not of the same order nor adapted to the same method of combat. The contest continued for more than a year, with preparations, advances, attacks, skirmishes and tactical modifications all contributing to the lively character of this high-handed struggle. Events seem to have occurred in approximately the following order. During Lent of 1139, William of Saint Thierry wrote to Bernard to inform him of the errors attributed to Abelard, based on propositions gathered from among his disciples. Bernard asked for clarifications and after Easter obtained an interview with William. Then he met with Abelard himself, as if to mitigate by human contact the harshness of the conflict already being waged on the level of ideas. During the last months of 1139, he composed his *Treatise Against the Errors of Abelard* addressed to Innocent II, and Letter 188 directed to the entire Roman Curia. For his part, Abelard published an *Apologia* and one of his disciples, an anonymous abbot, composed in his defense a clumsy tract entitled "Dispute". In January 1140, the controversy was intensified. Bernard dictated a series of letters, which Nicholas of Clairvaux had a hand in publishing, and he forwarded several to those cardinals whom he knew to be his supporters. Meanwhile, at Abelard's initiative, a confrontation between himself and Bernard was being prepared for the occasion of a bishops' meeting to be held at Sens at the beginning of June. It convened, but without the discussion. Abelard had invited his disciples to assist at this match where he expected brilliantly to crush the adversary. But the abbot of Clairvaux called the bishops together on the eve of the public session and with them, in Abelard's absence, prepared the morrow's performance: Abelard would present himself not as an orator, but as the accused. He would be allowed the opportunity to defend himself. Astonished, and probably also stricken with a physical ailment, Abelard refused to speak, appealed to Rome, and left. But Bernard anticipated him by means of letters resulting in confirmation of the sentence. Abelard was informed of this during his stopover at Cluny where Peter the Venerable lovingly received the old master, a humbled, weary and sick man. Peter assured him in one of his priories an honorable end to his life.

Thus ended the intellectual tournament which had brought together the two greatest minds of the time. In the writings extracted from both by the controversy, the violence of tone is extreme. Using invectives of a prophetic and apocalyptic language was part of the literary genre. Nevertheless, here again rhetoric does not explain everything, even if we take into account the part played by Nicholas of Clairvaux in the style of certain letters, for some of these were reviewed and corrected under Bernard's direction. Also, without a doubt, a comparison of this correspondence with those letters where St Jerome sketched the portrait of some of his enemies, sometimes after their death, demonstrates that spitefulness could go even further. It remains to say that this outburst of insults and accusations based on hasty denunciations reveals in St Bernard an unbridled passion. For their part, the prelates assembled at the tribunal of Sens perhaps made legitimate use of their doctrinal authority to the extent of their jurisdiction. But, after having accepted the debate proposed by Abelard—for which they were not prepared— they surely offered fresh proof of weakness in accepting the procedure improvised by the Abbot of Clairvaux. Did the Pope and some of his entourage not demonstrate a certain precipitancy in so quickly approving their decision? As for Abelard's silence at the time of his accusation, it can be interpreted as a sign of weakness, physical or moral, or of greatness. As always in these animated conflicts, where intellectual fervor in defending a truth believed to be threatened confers an absolute character on the opposition of persons and creates an impassioned atmosphere which is difficult for us to imagine, there were guilty parties on all sides. William of Saint Thierry was not among the least guilty.

In the affair which placed Bernard in opposition to Gilbert, Bishop of Poitiers, at the Council of Reims in 1148, several phases of the process at Sens were reenacted. Here again we cannot form a definitive judgment on the crux of the problem since some of Gilbert's important works have not been published. It seems that he too had been the victim of several of his disciples, since his teaching on several points was subtle. For him, as for Abelard, the question concerned "universals" and the way in which each being participates in the Being of God, qualified as "the form of all beings". Is there, and of what order is, a difference between God and his essence on the one hand, and on the other, between his essence and his attributes? Is God identical with "divinity"? The solution to these problems involved subtle distinctions and definitions on the subject of the good, of substance, of why a being is what it is, as well as many other notions difficult to formulate, and their consequences in relation to the mysteries of the Trinity and the Incarnation. Gilbert of Poitiers excelled in the realm of dialectic. He was a master in the art of the method, even if the application which he made to matters of faith could lead to conclusions which were not imperative or which raised difficulties, at least in the eyes of some.

Once again Bernard, perhaps conscious of his deficiencies in comparison with such a thinker, or desiring to mitigate the rigidity of speculative positions by means of a personal encounter, asked, through the agency of John of Salisbury, for a meeting with the bishop of Poitiers. Gilbert took the upper hand and suggested that the Abbot of Clairvaux would do better to seek instruction in the schools. On the eve of the Council, where Eugene III and the College of Cardinals were to be present, Bernard called together a group of French and English prelates favorable to him and had them approve propositions contrary to Gilbert's. This manoeuvre resulted in the indisposition of several cardinals. Gilbert defended himself and Bernard had to explain his behavior before the Pope. The bishop of Poitiers declared that he would loyally acquiesce to the faith of all and said that he was ready to correct his books. Warned but not condemned, he left the debate in an honorable fashion, and it was rather Bernard's reputation which was tarnished in some people's minds. Even with good intentions, had he not sought to abuse his prestige by anticipating and influencing the judgment of the tribunal which had, in the event, been organized by representatives of highest authority?

The evaluation proposed by two contemporaries reveals their hesitation before the mystery of a man at once so eminent and so disconcerting. The Cistercian chronicler and bishop, Otto of Freising, had to write:

> As for knowing whether, in this affair, the Abbot of Clairvaux, as a man, allowed himself to be deceived by the fragility of human weakness, or whether the Bishop, a shrewd and learned man, avoided sentence by dissembling his purpose—it is not for us to judge or debate.

He at least retained his admiration, despite their shortcomings, for both the saint and the scholar:

> Testimonies both old and new demonstrate that saints and wise men, in this flesh subject to corruption, often stumble into such failings (*fre-*

quenter in talibus fallantur).

After their death, John of Salisbury, who had attended the Council of Reims, continued to see Bernard as the specialist in "divine words" and Gilbert as the superior in "liberal disciplines". By different roads, they had sought the same goal and obtained "at last the definitive contemplation of the same truth."

The Second Crusade

The last great adventure in which Bernard involved himself was the Second Crusade. Before considering the spiritual interests at stake, we must briefly recall the facts. At Christmas in 1145, during the course of a Council held at Bourges in the presence of King Louis VII, there was talk of a Crusade to the Holy Land to rescue the French territory of Jerusalem which was threatened by an Arab thrust following upon the fall of Edessa the previous year. Bernard did not take part in this assembly. But soon, on March 1st, Eugene III issued a bull which was a call to arms and he commissioned the Abbot of Clairvaux to promote the venture. On 31 March, Bernard found himself at Vezelay beside the King, stirring up the people on behalf of this cause. Then he traveled through several French provinces where many people flocked to his cause. Aided by Nicholas of Clairvaux, he sent an encyclical letter to the temporal and spiritual leaders of various nations. In 1146 and 1147, he preached the "cause of Christ" in Flanders, then in Germany where he convinced the Emperor Conrad III to take up the Cross. He exerted himself to foster agreement among the princes. After two years of difficult preparations, the armies marched. Before arriving in the Holy Land they were decimated by the Turks. Kings and barons were divided, the battles lacked cohesion, the set-backs increased, and in July 1148, at the gates of Damascus, the Second Crusade failed once and for all. Abbot Suger of Saint Denis later planned to get a new expedition underway and captured St Bernard's interest. He in turn tried to convince Conrad and Eugene III—but in vain. At Chartres in May 1150, Bernard was designated by the bishops and knights as head of the Crusade, but the nomination remained ineffectual. Worse yet, some noblemen returning from the Orient blamed Bernard for their defeat and even went so far as to contest the donations they had made to Clairvaux before they left. The success of Bernard's preaching had been largely due to the fascination of his personality and his speech. Because of this, he felt the final disappointment all the more vividly.

What conception had he formed of the different categories of men affected by this venture? The infidels, that is, the pagans who were the enemy in this case, he simply compared to obstinate sinners—the common view at the time—because he believed that they all had supposedly refused the opportunity of hearing the Gospel proclaimed. During this period, there were only vague notions of their number and their religious situation. An exception was the Abbot of Cluny, Peter the Venerable, who decided to promote a better understanding of Islam by having the Koran translated. Bernard, whom he tried to associate in this effort of comprehension, did not respond. It was not that he lacked interest in the salvation of the infidels. In his very first treatise, *On the Degrees of Humility*, he had noted that, while the Church does not pray publicly for hardened sinners, "she prays with confidence for Jews, for heretics [and] for pagans" on Good Friday. And in Book III of his *Consideration*, written after the failure of the Crusade, he opened up new, purely apostolic, perspectives for Eugene III by reminding him of his duty to be a missionary, even to the infidels. But in this immediate situation these pagans appeared as enemies. Along with all his contemporaries, Bernard believed it necessary first to dominate them by force, not in order to convert them by this means, which he declared illegitimate, but to prevent them from jeopardizing christians.

It was on the occasion of the Crusade that he was led to take on the defense of the Jews. In the Rhineland, a certain Rudolph (Rasul), who claimed to be a monk, had taken it upon himself to preach a German Crusade and had unleashed a persecution against them. Bernard, consulted in the matter

by the Bishop of Mainz, rose up against this anti-semitism
and in an encyclical sent to all of the princes wrote:

> The Jews should not be persecuted, nor put to
> death, nor even banished. Consult the pages of
> Sacred Scripture. I know of a prophecy contained
> in one of the Psalms which concerns them: 'God,
> says the Church, has given me a lesson on the
> subject of my enemies: do not kill them, for fear
> that my people will forget me.' They are like
> living words and represent to us the Passion of the
> Lord. They have been dispersed throughout all
> nations so that, by suffering the just punishment
> of so great a crime, they might serve as witnesses
> to our redemption. (Letter 363)

And after these words, in conformity with the ideas of his
time, Bernard recalled that, according to the Apostle Paul,
"when the multitude of Gentiles shall have entered the
Church, then shall all of Israel be saved." And he concluded
that, without a doubt, if these too, in the present situation,
were acting as enemies, it was the princes' duty to repress
them by force.

> But it is proper to christian piety, if it lowers the
> mighty, to spare the vanquished, especially those
> who have received the promise of the law, who are
> descendants of our fathers, to whose number
> belonged, according to the flesh, the Christ who is
> blessed for all ages.

With christians of the Eastern Churches the problem was
different. What was Bernard's opinion there? He summarized the Eastern position to the Roman Church in one
terse phrase: *"Iuncti fide, pace divisi*; United by faith, they
are divided as to peace." And this not merely for lack of
ecclesiastical communion, but by reason of political rivalries,
especially between the Byzantines and the Franks in the Holy
Land. One of Bernard's illusions was his belief that the
Crusade would offer an occasion for reuniting the Churches
by having all christians struggle against a common enemy. In

order to curry the favor of Emperor Manuel I Comnenus, he
sent him the eldest son—not yet dubbed knight—of Count
Thibaut of Champagne, on whose territory Clairvaux was
located, and requested that he himself equip the boy for
battle. It was largely a matter of assuring that troops coming
from the West could cross the Empire. Manuel offered
security, but his promises were not kept. King Roger of
Sicily, for his part, ravaged the Greek possessions of the
Eastern Mediterranean in the summer of 1147. Thus besides
the divisions among the Latin countries, there now existed
others between them and the Byzantines. After the failure of
the Crusade, resulting from all of these weak points, the King
and Queen of France, on pilgrimage to Jerusalem, were
attacked on their return by the ships of Manuel Comnenus.
Even while such contrary interests and mutual misunder-
standing made any agreement impossible, Eugene III,
Bernard, and other religious leaders continued to believe that
the union of the Churches could be achieved, and they said as
much. The Abbot of Clairvaux reminded the Pope that he
belonged to all, "to Jews, Greeks, and Gentiles." He himself penetrated as far as possible into Greek theological
thought. Geoffrey of Auxerre would later say that he enjoyed
a great reputation "in the Eastern Church", and Anselm of
Havelberg would affirm that his sanctity was venerated "from
the West to the East." They undoubtedly recognized that,
despite illusions and perhaps some tactlessness, he had felt
himself responsible for all: infidels, Jews, and separated
christians.

Finally, what significance did he give to the Crusade for
Catholics themselves? For those who were "believers in
name only" and for sinners—that is, for all—he saw an
occasion of salvation: a means of loving the Lord and proving
it. A chance was offered to all those who wished to form or
to renew a personal relationship with God for the matter at
hand involved love of and service to Christ. Bernard had,
so-to-speak, "interiorized" the Crusade and its justification.
What had previously been merely a warlike expedition for
political ends became with him and under his influence and

example an act of penance, a step toward conversion. The holy war, if undertaken solely for the purpose of serving the Lord's "cause", of suffering and perhaps dying for him, became a means and an occasion for making one's peace with God: as an indulgence it bestowed pardon, as a pilgrimage it sanctified, as a possible martyrdom it offered reward.

This moral and purely religious conception of the Crusade exacted from all those involved complete purity of intention. The facts show that this disinterestedness was not the case with many of the leaders of the venture. They had had a difficult time reaching agreement during their preparations; then they had departed by different ways, some by land, others by sea; on the field of combat, their divisions were merely aggravated. After the inevitable defeat, Bernard, the accused, made an examination of conscience at the beginning of the second book of the *Consideration* which says a great deal about their dispositions and his own:

> In order to punish our sins, the Lord seems to have judged the world prematurely: with complete fairness certainly, but as if he no longer remembered his mercy. He has not spared his people and not even his Name; for do not the pagans say: 'Where is their God?' This is not surprising: the children of the Church, those who bear the name of christian, have been beaten in the desert where they have perished by the sword or have died of hunger. Discord ran rampant among their leaders, and the Lord allowed them to stray far off the paths. Ruin and misfortune were met along the way. Fear, confusion, and sadness invaded even the hearts of their kings. What humiliation for those who announced peace, for those who announced happiness! We have said: 'Here is peace', and there is no peace. We have promised happiness, and all are troubled.... Why then have we fasted if He has not looked down upon us? Why have we humbled ourselves by doing penance since he has not acknowledged it? But his fury

has still not turned from us, his hand is still raised against us.... Patiently he listens to the sacrilegious voices, the blasphemies of the Egyptians, who say that he has betrayed his own, leading them into the desert that they might be killed. Everyone knows: all of his decisions are in accord with the truth. Nevertheless, this latter is so profound an abyss that I believe I can say: 'Blessed are those who will not be scandalized...'

But by what right would a foolhardy man dare to find fault with that which he cannot understand? Let us remember similar judgments which God brought to bear in ages past; here we will find consolation: the same faults have merited the same punishments.... As for myself, it means little to me if I am judged by those who call evil good and good evil, who make darkness light and light darkness. If one or the other must occur, I prefer to see the murmurings of men rise up against me rather than against God. Voluntarily I take on the reproaches, the blasphemies, so that they will not reach as far as God. I find it good that he wishes to use me as his shield. I do not refuse to be without glory, as long as God's glory is not attacked.

This page full of emotion and of greatness reveals to us the depths of Bernard's soul. After his conversion, he had experienced the temptation to power. He knew the power of influence, success, even prestige, and a dangerous glory. He suffered from this duality within himself: the monk vowed to total detachment, the contemplative called to seek God alone; and the man of action, involved in public affairs, with political obligations. He often complained about it and referred to himself as the "chimera of my times, living neither as a cleric nor as a layman." He spoke of having been tempted to escape. As he wrote to Innocent II: "My soul is sorrowful to the point of flight." He confided to Eskil, the Archbishop of Lund: "I am torn asunder, distracted: I can take no more."

(Letter 390) Thus he never consented utterly to power. He remained tormented by his solicitude for God and for his Church, even though he sometimes employed methods which could be considered as not the only possible means, nor even legitimate.

Throughout his entire career, in his most diverse activity, the important place held in his work by the thought of Clairvaux is undeniable. Perhaps the most continuous current in his life was his concern to work for the reform of the Church, which he conceived primarily as an interior reform and thus only able to be accomplished within the souls of men, and not by institutions alone. As a monk, he sought to contribute to this endeavor through the work of monasteries, especially Cistercian and preferably, but not exclusively, descended from Clairvaux. This kind of obsession led him to found, develop, and propagate Cistercian abbeys everywhere, and inspired a political view destined to place Cistercian monks in important posts. Did he do this through a desire for domination, through ambition on his own behalf and on that of his brothers? This should not necessarily be presumed; in each case it would have to be proven. He himself speaks of his desire for reform and sanctity. His goal was an exalted one. His means may have appeared less so in the eyes of some of his contemporaries or of historians: this passionate man may have acted blindly.

God undertook to purify him by failure. The lack of success, which he felt all the more grievously because it was public and was accompanied by a moral downfall, was the disaster which, from the beginning, cast gloom on the Crusade which he had prepared with such love and with the evident help of God. While preaching it, especially in the Rhineland, he had worked miracles that were spoken of by all and had awakened confidence in the Lord. Should we reproach him for not having condemned from the start this war which, like any other, would entail suffering, disorder, and misery? This would be an unfair imposition of the values of one era onto another, and a judgment made according to a psychology which was unknown at the time. It would also be forgetting that, for him, what counted was not so much the success as the effort. In his preaching before the Crusade, as in his examination of conscience after the defeat, he declared that the important point was not whether one had attained victory, but whether one profitted from the opportunity offered by God, and had responded to his grace by a true conversion of the heart. If this was true, and for those for whom it was true, nothing was lost. Bernard was not a statesman whose initiatives could be judged according to their effectiveness in military, political, or economic realms. He was a spokesman for Jesus Crucified. Thus he was also in character when he experienced humiliation, when he proclaimed that renunciation and love triumph over power.

Prologus in antyphona[ria]

cisstcienses

Humilis ab[...]
lis. omnib[us ...]
hoc antyp[...]
cantaturis [...]

· cetera que op[...]
sunt patres nři. cistcienses[...]
inchoatores. hoc q̇ studiosi[...]
giosissime curauimt: ut in e[...]

BERNARD'S MESSAGE

A T THE SAME TIME BERNARD TOOK ACTION he was also speaking. Of his spoken words we know almost nothing. But we do have the writings whereby he exercised influence in his own times as well as after his death and up to our own day. They are the expression of a doctrine. Bernard was not a pious author who appealed to sentiment in order to deliver facile, delicate exhortations. He was a man with an exceptional intellectual gift, a man of God, enriched by special graces, who placed all of his talents at the service of his reflection on matters of faith: he was a theologian. Was he also a mystic? He has always been considered one. But this poses a problem which must be stated clearly before we can further probe his thought.

More than once Bernard referred to something called "experience" as a necessary source for any knowledge of the divine mysteries. He either presumed it in his reader or wished to call it forth. The word and its connotations are linked with what it called "mysticism". The meaning of this term has been much disputed. Today it is generally accepted that a mystic is one who has a certain experience of God, whatever may be the content, the accompanying psychological phenomena, and any analysis which can be made. In its most exalted form, this experience is "ecstasy", which St Bernard also referred to as a going out of oneself, *excessus*. The soul is raised beyond the ordinary use of her faculties because God has entered and taken possession of her whole being—a "visitation" by the Most High. Bernard declared that he had personal experience of this condition:

> I admit it: the Word has come to me, many times. Often he has entered into me and sometimes I have not been immediately aware of his arrival: but I perceived that he was there and I remember his presence. Even when I had a presentiment of it, I could never have the sensation of the exact moment of his entrance or of his departure. Whence did he come into my soul? Where did he go when leaving it? How did he enter and leave? Even now I must confess that I do not know...
>   (Sermon 74 on The Song of Songs, 5)

What could be more transparently sincere than this confidence, this confession, made in the first person singular, by a witness who says "I" and speaks of himself? However, if we read the passage from Origen on which this page depends, we find the following:

> As God is my witness, I have often seen the Spouse coming and resting in me and then leaving quite suddenly: and I could no longer find him whom I sought. Then I desired his return and occasionally he did come back; then, when he has thus appeared to me and allowed himself to be seized by my hands, he disappears again and once more I begin to search for him. This has happened many times....

Even better than a comparison of the two translations, the Latin texts of these two confessions prove that Bernard drew his inspiration from Origen and used some of the very same expressions. As usual, however, he did not copy: he transformed his source and enriched it by his great literary talent. We at least have a right to ask wherein lies the sincerity, the actual experience behind this admirable rhetoric. All Bernard's work raises this same problem. Must we give up all attempts at understanding the depths of his soul? The task would still be difficult, but we do have his doctrine, stated with such constancy and inner coherence that it indubitably reveals his most profound and unswerving convictions. In this sense, his doctrine teaches us about his experience and would not have existed without this experience. Thus there will always be two elements in his theological method and the teachings which result from it: the effort of the intelligence reflecting on the objective facts of faith and the recourse to his own personal life as it confronted these revealed truths. This aspect of intimacy and subjective experience occasionally obscured the clarity of his statements on truths which could have been handled by his reason; but it does much to enhance, we might say, the prime matter which theology seeks to elaborate. Theology can never be pure speculation. It retains something of the obscurity of faith and respects its mystery.

Nevertheless, this experience, which cannot be separated from reflection, does not result only, even primarily, from elevated mystical states. It springs from a dual awareness: the everyday mediocrity of man feeling the weight of his nature, and the fervor possible for the christian and the monk ardently pursuing his vocation. It is accomplished in daily life, in the midst of a community of religious who participate in the same wretchedness and the same grace, who all suffer the same humiliations and all strive to rise to contemplative prayer. Bernard's theology is "monastic" insofar as it is lived, realized by an abbot and his sons, and explained for their benefit. The amazing thing is that, at the same time, it is universal because these seekers of God are merely the "specialists" in an occupation which is essential to the Church and to each of her members.

We can say that all of St Bernard's doctrine is centered on three main themes: sin, Christ, and the Church.

Man the Sinner

The first experience offered for our consideration is our condition as sinners. Bernard did not linger here in a lengthy analysis. He was not what would be called today an

introvert: he does not speak of himself, he does not describe.
He often said briefly what he felt, but he reflected on it in
faith. He made theology out of his own circumstances and
personal history. This was not, as with St Augustine, the
history of a convert who emerged slowly from a long
existence spent far from God. It is simply the experience of a
monk. The meditation of the contemplative gave him the
time and the opportunity to be lucid about himself, and a
perusal of Sacred Scripture helped him understand the significance of his experience. Bernard was aware of his gifts.
Letter 372 to the Bishop of Palencia develops the theme of
the gratitude one should have toward the Creator for the
talents and graces which we owe him. But he added that
humility is not inconsistent with a recognition of our own
worth. On the contrary, it makes recognition possible.
Humility is located on another, much deeper level. It is
nothing other than the awareness of our need for God. Such
is the "truth" of our condition: without God we can do
nothing for God, and, since we are created for him, we cannot even be completely ourselves without him.

God has made us in his "image" and "likeness". The
first of these two favors is particularly manifest in the fact
that we are endowed with free will. Inherent in our very
nature, this gift is inalienable. Nevertheless, the "likeness"
was a grace which confirmed our freedom by adherence to
the will of God; it was an added gift which could be lost, and
in fact was lost by sin: man strayed into the "region of
dissimilitude". In him, because of his original and personal
sin, the "likeness" to God has been erased; at the same
time, the "image" has been altered, but it has not been
completely destroyed. God has loved, sought, and saved his
creation by sending his own Son to earth. The exile has been
recalled, the crooked has been made straight. Man still
retains that vestige of his original rectitude which gave him
an aptitude for doing good, which remained in him as a
spontaneous protest against evil. The grace of Christ has re-
established the "likeness" and restored the "image". Nevertheless, man is still injured. From his sinful condition, he

retains the wounds which Bernard compared to scars that have healed but are still painful. He is now constantly divided between his supernatural capacity for God and his natural weight pulling him away from God. To evoke the wretchedness of our condition, Bernard used expressions as profound as those of Paschal. Even redeemed, even sanctified, even called to the "paradise of the cloister", man is dull and mediocre. Bernard estimated that many of his monks lived in "apathy, aridity, torpor", and nearly "degradation" (*hebetudo stolidae mentis:* we hesitate to translate such strong expressions).

Still, the abbot of Clairvaux and his monks maintained a confidence which was all the greater as the experience of their misery was more profound. In the same text where he described the mediocrity of his monks—and what must it be like in places where the abbot is not a Bernard!—he also bore witness to their desire for God, their efforts to reach him, and their union with him in hope. He believed in man's nobility even as sinner. "We are noble creatures, we have greatness of soul: *Nobiles enim creaturae sumus, et magni cuisdam animi...,*" he writes in his fourth Sermon for the Ascension. Humility does not stifle magnanimity. The whole process of "conversion" throughout the entire life of every man—which, for the monk, is not immediately achieved upon his arrival in the cloister—consists in liberating the true self which is made in the likeness of God, in purifying the self from all egoism, and in acquiring, preserving and nurturing the life of God within the self. The will, wounded by sin and turned in upon itself, spontaneously seeks its own interest instead of the glory of God and the welfare of neighbor. Grace and asceticism must replace this "selfish will" with a "communal will" which seeks the general good, the good of all, under all of its forms. This is charity, a participation in God's own love.

This conception of man and his relationship with God sprang from an experience which every man can have and from the Scriptures which every christian can read. Certainly this type of anthropology borrows some elements of its vocabulary from ancient philosophical systems. But is this the same as saying that it is platonic, and therefore marked by a degree of pessimism and engendering a need for compensation and purification? These simplistic points of view are not confirmed by current research by historians of medieval thought, or by an objective reading of St Bernard's works. The explanation must be sought primarily in the Psalms, in the Gospels, in St Paul, and in the rest of the two Testaments. For example, the abbot of Clairvaux did not locate concupiscence in the instincts of the "flesh", as if the materiality of the body created an insurmountable dualism between senses and spirit; rather he saw it situated in the "heart", in the sense that this word is used in the Bible (which is also close to the meaning given it by modern psychology): an intimate center where all the tendencies and aspirations of the soul meet and struggle with one another, the lower with the higher. At the point of departure of the spiritual itinerary whose stages Bernard marked out, there is "fear of the Lord", as it is understood in the Bible. Not a depressing terror, but that knowledge of self, that awareness of man's wretchedness, which is the beginning of wisdom. When a man understands his own miserable condition, he knows that it is the same for every man and he has compassion for his brothers. He forgives. Bernard later wrote in Letter 70: "If it were a sin to have mercy, I could not prevent myself from being merciful, even by a firm act of the will." He felt that the common life of the monastery offered privileged conditions for the accomplishment of this progressive liberation from all egoism. Humility, fraternal compassion, and prayer lead the monk gradually from an experience of his own truth—which is his wretchedness—to the contemplation of God's truth, which is love, and God's mercy which has been revealed in Christ.

Christ the Saviour

For Bernard, in fact, the solution to man's problem lay in Christ, in whom "mercy" has taken precedence over "misery", in whom God has been reconciled with his sinful creation. Bernard applied the words of a Psalm to this

mystery: "Mercy and truth have met, justice and peace have
embraced." We cannot summarize Bernard's Christology in
a few pages without depriving it of its fullness and precision.
We are content here with pointing out some of the main
themes.

Christ is the Saviour of man because he is the perfect
realization of what man should be in the presence of God. He
is the ideal man, the one who gives meaning to human
existence. He is perfectly man and, besides, he is so perfectly united to God that he is God-Man. As Word, he is the
image of the Father; as Incarnate Word, he is the image of
man reconciled with the Father. He is the model that must
be imitated. Bernard said this a number of times in words
borrowed from St Paul: he is the "form" to whom
"deformed" man must "conform" in order to be "reformed". The aim of the Incarnation was to reveal the
Father and communicate the Spirit, but also to show men the
way by which they can return to the Father in the Spirit. For
carnal man, God is invisible and unattainable; he has made
himself accessible in Jesus. By assuming our nature, by
having compassion for our wretched state and personally
experiencing it, Christ has renewed our confidence. The
Incarnation was necessary so that he could become our
Mediator. It was a communication of the Holy Spirit which
prepared Mary for motherhood, granting her fullness of
grace, freeing her from sin—Bernard and nearly all of his
contemporaries thought that she was not exempt—helping
her to believe that the power of the Most High could make a
virgin conceive, making her fruitful, accomplishing in her the
union of humanity and divinity. In Christ's personal unity,
these three substances, the Word, the soul, and the body are
joined. Bernard understood this union between God and
human nature as a union of love, an active, continual, and
indestructible consent. Because of the incomparable and
eternal love of the Most High for the human nature which he
had predestined for himself, and because of the presence of
the divinity of the Word, this union, unlike that of body and
soul in man, would resist death. The Son of God willed to

experience a real death, but one in which and after which the Word would remain united to the body and soul of the Son of Man.

Thus the Incarnation conferred on Jesus the fullness of divinity; it made him the Head of all humanity, commissioned to communicate his grace to all those who looked on him as their Mediator. It also planted in Him, and consequently in us, the seed of the Resurrection. By means of the Incarnation, the Word assumed and sanctified not only man's nature, but his destiny—to return to God and be glorified with Him. The glorification of Jesus, accomplished at the time of his Resurrection and Ascension, transferred his humanity from our own human condition to the divine condition. All that is human remains in Jesus, but is transformed in glory, transfigured, and, as as been written, "trans-situated" into the very life of God. Contemplating Jesus in the triumph of his Ascension, Bernard spoke to him in his second sermon for Pentecost:

> The man which you had assumed is now included
> in the very identity of the divinity (*susceptum
> hominem in ipsa divinitatis claudis identitate.*)

Once glorified, Jesus fully became the Saviour and Redeemer, celestial man and first-born of a new race, the principle—that is, the beginning—of resurrection for those who pass with him from the flesh to the spirit. God's descent in the humanity of Jesus thus results in humanity's ascent toward God: first in Jesus, and then in those who adhere to his teachings. At the end of time, on the day of wrath, he will come as judge, but also as a brother to the humanity which he willed to redeem and to whom he revealed the mercy of the Father:

> Oh true Father of mercies! He wills that men be
> judged by a man so that, in the midst of such
> great terror and so many evils, the likeness of a
> similar nature might give confidence to the elect!

Even now, the redeemed who participate in the Spirit sent

after his glorification are, in the obscurity of faith but in actual fact, associated with him in his new condition.

This rapid recollection of the mystery of Jesus as conceived by Bernard in accordance with Scripture, notably St John and St Paul with the Fathers of the Church—perhaps especially with the Greeks, and with the liturgy, explains several characteristic traits of his teaching. First of all, it emphasizes the importance which he attributed to the feast of the Ascension. It is one of the feasts that he most often spoke of because it is the beginning, and something like a symbol, of christian detachment: a continual passage from Christ according to the flesh to Christ according to the Spirit, a progress in an obscure and unifying faith. This traditional conception of the mystery of Redemption also helps us understand Bernard's insistence on the imitation of Jesus: This theme serves to explain his teaching on grace, the sacraments, and asceticism. It is connected with the doctrine of the image of God in such a way that there is a remarkable cohesion in this whole assembly of ideas, despite the poetic and not very systematic character of many of the texts in which they are expounded.

For man, conversion is a matter of returning to the Father through the Son, in the Spirit. As second Person of the Trinity, the Son is the perfect image of the Father, and it is in conformity with him that man was created, image of the image, reflection of the Word who is a reflection of the Father. Henceforth, to be assimilated by Christ is to recover the image and likeness of the Father. Jesus came to restore the life of grace by the mysteries he accomplished and the examples he offered. We must therefore both imitate him and participate in the sacraments which communicate his life to us. He imitated us in our human condition so that we might be able to imitate him, in some way at least. During his life on earth, there were manifestations of his glory and power. We can only admire these, and we should do so. But what we can and must imitate are those manifestations of his gentleness and his humility. Bernard does not usually dwell

on the circumstances of Jesus' earthly existence. He recalls
briefly the poverty of his birth, his obedience, his fasting, his
temptation and his patience before the incomprehension of
the multitudes, the leaders of the people, and even his own
disciples; his compassion toward Lazarus, his nights spent in
prayer, his silence during the trial, and his sorrowful death:
in a word, the proofs that he gave of his goodness, all that he
"did" to illustrate what he "taught" concerning the need to
forgive and to lay down one's life. He always united word
and example: he began by accomplishing what he taught.
Bernard liked to refer to this by citing words from the Acts of
the Apostles: *Coepit Iesus facere et locere.* And by his very
actions, our salvation was realized. Bernard did not attempt
an analysis of the Lord's soul, he offered little description of
his sufferings, he did not exercise his imagination. He went
immediately to the mysteries which these events contain and
reveal. All of this happened for us. By what means can we
take possession of it?

We must first of all "represent" these mysteries to
ourselves by meditation on the Scriptures. This is the role of
"devotion" and "memory". But this mental activity is not
enough. We must also participate in the objective reality of
these events by celebrating their efficacious commemoration
in the liturgy and by receiving the sacraments which
communicate the grace won for us; we must thereby
assimilate these events into our whole being, into every area
of our activity. By this ritual of worship, they acquire a
"presence" which is both a remembrance of their historical
achievement and an expectation of their complete manifes-
tation. This anticipation is like a "memory of the future"
(*memoria futurorum*). It maintains in us the desire to be
ultimately united one day to Jesus in the glory of the Father
and encourages us along the path of humility, which is the
only way that leads to him. If there can be no imitation of
Christ without a reception of the sacraments, it is because the
acts of Jesus were at the same time examples and
mysteries—that is, *sacramenta*, in the sense that this word
was used by St Paul, the Fathers, and the liturgy. From this

fact springs Bernard's insistence on the necessity of eating
the body and drinking the blood of the Son of God, and of
receiving pardon for our sins, which included the ritual of
footwashing.   Of all these sacraments, the first and "the
beginning was Baptism which has rooted us in a likeness to
Jesus' death", and which associates us with his risen life.

Thus, in the teaching of St Bernard, there is a sacramental
realism which avoids a type of "devotion" that is only
sentimental activity, and an imitation that is only human and
illusory effort.   In particular, the Eucharist, joined to
exercises of prayer and asceticism, assures the indwelling of
God in man and helps the christian to suppress his evil tendencies, to purify his memory, rectify his intentions, and
make progress in the faith.   It brings light for his intellect
and strength for his will; it confers a pledge of the resurrection to come.   All of this teaching, solid and fervent,
having little affective quality is expressed particularly in
Bernard's sermons for the liturgical year, most especially in
those which treat the Paschal mystery.   Bernard did not yield
to sensory and imaginative piety: he accepted its legitimacy,
but felt one must go beyond it.   Like the Apostles on the day
of the Ascension, christians must learn to live apart from the
visible humanity of Jesus, he believed like Paul, they must be
able to say: "If we have known Christ according to the flesh,
now it is no longer thus that we know him."   As Origen had
done a number of times, they must be able to apply to Jesus
these words from *Lamentations*:   "The Lord Christ is Spirit
before our faces: we live in his shadow among the nations."

Nor did Bernard seek exalted experiences of an intellectual
order, a kind of bodiless encounter with pure truth.   In his
sermon for the first Sunday of November, in which he
comments on these words of Isaiah: "I saw the Lord seated
on his throne of glory", and which constitutes a treatise on
the vision of God, he continually turned his attention to the
mysteries of Christ (and we know the realism of his conception), to man's need to conform his will to God's by
mortifying his flesh, by acquiring humility and meekness of
heart, and by imitating Jesus.   When he was questioned

concerning the extraordinary revelations and ecstasies of St Hildegarde, he demonstrated his prudence, and even a certain reserve: he dwelt on generalities and recalled the law of humility. In a word, Bernard's spirituality is centered on the Incarnation. The body he held in high esteem, in the christian as well as in Christ Himself. It allowed our Head to manifest the invisible mercy of the Father; it helps his members to acquire an understanding of the faith, to love the Lord with their whole heart, according to their own nature, occasionally to arrive at an intuitive perception—but not one produced without mental images—of supernatural truths, and especially to penetrate the content and efficacy of the mysteries of salvation within the human condition.

The Church

Where will this encounter between sinful man and Christ the Saviour take place? Bernard replies: in the Church. Even more, the Church *is* this very encounter. She is the mystery of salvation communicated to men and realized in them; she is the union of the redeemed with God in the Holy Spirit whom Jesus has sent, and she is the communion of all those who participate in this same Spirit. The symbols which best express the essence of the Church are those which evoke the intimate union between two beings and those which speak of love, marriage, and embracing. When Bernard commented on the Song of Songs, he was thinking of this spouse who is the Church. The betrothals and espousals of ancient times prepared and prefigured her, while those of which the Apocalypse sings will be her perfect accomplishment. Here on earth, the Church is already in faith the heavenly spouse of the Incarnate Word. She is not yet clothed in the glory of the Resurrection, but she already receives, possesses, and shares in the Spirit who sanctifies. All of the other biblical symbols illustrate this sanctifying function of the Church: she is the Temple and City of God, she is the true Jerusalem, she is the choice vine described by the prophets. Because she has been sanctified by the presence of God, she in turn sanctifies by communicating this presence.   Bernard

conceived of the Church before all else as a society for
sanctification. Here again, he thought as a monk: if the aim
of the christian life is to seek a personal relationship with God
such as the conditions of life in the cloister would tend to
foster, the Church is like one vast monastery, and the abbot
of Clairvaux referred to his community as the spouse of the
Word, Jerusalem, the Temple of God, and the vine of Israel.

Although spiritual and already eternal, the universal
Church and the local community of God-seekers live in space
and in time: they have a body. In his sermons *On the
Dedication of a Church*, Bernard managed to harmonize all of
these realities in a way that demonstrated his rare poetical
depth, but he said nothing about the beauty of the building
made of stone. Fontenay and other claravallian abbeys give
evidence of his concern for the esthetic in architecture. But
the building is merely a support, a symbol: the true mystery
is the life lived within. The entire institutional structure is at
the service of the interior life.

All those to whom God communicates his holiness are the
Church, and they are among the first of the blessed souls.
Bernard did not hesitate to say that Christ is in some way
their Saviour, and that they are the first to realize the role of
Christ's spouse. He saw such a continuity between the
earthly Church and the heavenly Church—both constituting
the unique spouse of the Incarnate Word—that he showed
how the Church here below is constatnly assisted by the one
on high in her struggle against evil, in her prayer, and in all
that she does to unite herself to the One she loves and whose
love has benefitted all.

Among all human creatures, the one who has received
privileged grace is the Virgin Mary. Like all those who have
commented on the mystery of Christ, Bernard was drawn to
mention her very often. But he rarely spoke of her in a
systematic way. He did so in several admirable pages of
biblical poetry and human emotion which have been
reproduced many times and have become part of the clergy's
breviary: their literary quality and the ease with which they
harmonized with current devotion merited this honor for

them.   But we cannot use them as a basis for judging
Bernard's marian doctrine.   His teaching is hardly original:
much less so than St Anselm's in the preceding generation
or, in Bernard's own time, than Anselm's disciples' such as
Eadmer or the anonymous author of a treatise on the
Assumption circulated under the name of St Augustine.   In
the only case where Bernard wished to devote himself to
precise argumentation on a point of mariology, on the
question of the Virgin's sinless conception, he did so to sustain a widespread opinion which was beginning to be
questioned by some of the better theologians whose intuitions
and reasonings would later be confirmed by the dogma of the
Immaculate Conception.   The problem is complex and its
history during St Bernard's time has given rise to subtle controversies.   There have been attempts to cast doubt on the
authenticity of the famous Letter 174 where Bernard
reproaches the Canons of Lyon for celebrating the feast of
Mary's conception.   Honesty obliges us to recognize that, on
this occasion, the Abbot of Clairvaux was defending a lost
cause.   There is some merit for him in the fact that his very
opposition provoked the development of theological reflection.

However, Bernard's true greatness as a witness to the
Church's marian devotion is situated on another plane.   His
role in this area was not of innovating, but of maintaining an
awareness of certain traditions in the religious reflection of
his times; without these, all doctrinal progress would have
been rootless and perhaps even dangerous.   His testimony of
the ancient manner of conceiving the mystery of Mary retains
all of its value.   Even in our own days, it has stirred up
renewed interest.   Instead of insisting on the personal
privileges of the Virgin Mary, Bernard concentrated on her
role in the work of salvation.   In agreement with Sacred
Scriptures, the Fathers of the Church and the liturgy, he
situated the mystery of divine motherhood within the whole
context of the Incarnation, its preparations and its effects. For
example, at the beginning of his treatise *On the Praises of
the Virgin Mary*, he only spoke of Mary after having first
praised and honored her Son and after having recalled the

entire evolution of God's redemptive plan. Mary was always in a position secondary to Christ and Bernard did not feel that he was failing in love toward the Mother of God by his greater contemplation of her Son. The Virgin was the means by which God accomplished his designs; this explains Bernard's stress, when speaking of Mary, on the symbols and characters of the Old Testament who had announced and prefigured her. He did not separate her from Christ and the Church. As Mother of God, she became mother of all the sons of God; her virginal motherhood was granted her with a view to the salvation of the entire human race. She is the most perfect realization of God's Israel, she is the model and symbol of the chosen and redeemed people, she is the example of achieved sanctification which was the goal of the Old and New Covenants and which is accomplished in the Church. From this point of view, Bernard's mariology, like his ecclesiology, was monastic: the virtues of the Virgin Mary which he admired and offered for our imitation are humility, obedience, the spirit of silence, recollection, a taste for intimate prayer, and striving toward a personal union with God in love.

Because the mystery of the redemptive Incarnation is at the core of Scripture, St Bernard's marian writings are undoubtedly richer in biblical themes than all of his other works. But he also praised Mary in another language, applying to her the feudal vocabulary of the time: she is "queen", "advocate", "mediatrix"; she "reconciles", "represents", "recommends" all men to her Son. Before the Judge, she is the "mother of mercy", she supports the "cause" of our salvation, she intervenes in the "trial" which places us in opposition to God. It is important that we fully understand these many expressions. In reality, everything that comes from the Almighty Father comes through the Son who is like Him. But this Son has willed to communicate himself to men by the mediation of Mary who was truly his mother. And all of the gifts that God gives to the world through his Son continue to pass through Mary. She is indeed the universal intermediary and, according to a favorite expression of Bernard, the "mediatrix". She has been placed between God and us to facilitate our relations with God. She is very close to us and takes us by the hand, but she is likewise very close to Christ and she reunites us with him, she leads us to him. This is why we can have an unlimited confidence in her: she presents all of our needs to her Son and then transmits to us all of the graces which he sends. Bernard developed this idea by means of the charming comparison of the "aquaduct": eternal life is the inexhaustible spring which waters the entire surface of the redeemed world. This fountain of life is Christ himself, our Lord. His fullness was, in a sense, emptied to become our forgiveness when he hid his glory beneath the humiliation of his humanity. By the Redemption, the waters of this fountain were diverted in our direction. This stream of heavenly water has come down to us by an aquaduct which dispenses grace on each of us according to our needs. This aquaduct is Mary whom the Angel called "full of grace": admirable aquaduct which reaches to the highest heavens, to the very heart of God, and descends to the most intimate center of our hearts. As long as Mary did not exist, God's grace was not so abundantly poured out on humanity. But since Mary became the Mother of the Mediator, she is the mediatrix who overwhelms us with his grace. If the majesty of God dazzles us, if the infinite glory of Jesus Christ gives us the impression that he is too far away from us, Mary should give us confidence: "The Son will hearken to the Mother, and the Father will hearken to the Son."

In the sermons which Bernard wrote for the solemn feasts of the saints, he emphasized their virtues more than their miracles. We may admire the marvels retold in their legends, which Bernard treats with considerable reserve, but we must above all stand in awe of their examples and imitate them. Their role in the continuing history of the people of God—and this applies also to his contemporaries like Malachy O'Morghair—is to prove that the mystery of holiness which is the Church can be realized to an intense degree in human natures like our own. The saint that Bernard spoke of most

often was St Joseph, and he did so in strict accordance with
the Bible, ignoring the apocryphal accounts. As would many
others later, he praised his faith, his chastity, and his
humility. But even more than this, adhering to a patristic
tradition which dated from the time of Origen, he elaborated
Joseph's significance in the history of salvation and his role
in the Church. He understood that the importance accorded
to Mary's spouse by St Luke in his accounts of Jesus' infancy
should be interpreted with reference to the patriarch of the
same name spoken of in Genesis:

> The ancient Joseph, sold because of his brothers'
> jealousy and led into Egypt, prefigures Christ, sold
> by Judas; the second Joseph, to escape the
> jealousy of Herod, brought Christ into Egypt....To
> the former was given an understanding of the
> mystery of dreams, and to the latter, a knowledge
> and share in the secrets of heaven. The former
> gathered in a surplus of wheat, not for himself
> alone but for a whole people; the latter received in
> trust the living Bread, as much for himself as for
> the entire world...He is at once the faithful and
> prudent servant whom the Lord chose as support
> for his mother, foster father for himself, and
> finally as a unique and perfectly faithful cooperator
> in his great designs on earth. (*On the Praises of
> the Virgin Mary* II, 16)

A descendant of David, Joseph received the privilege of his
ancestor so as to be, like a "second David", the confidant
and witness of the accomplishment of the promise (ibid.). He
was present at the circumcision in his role as father and
spouse; at the Presentation, he "offered to the Lord not his
own son, but the true Son of the Lord". He was the one who
had received an angel's revelation concerning the significance
of the name of Jesus: "He will save His people from their
sins." Therefore, Joseph is, after Mary, the most perfect
realization of the mystery of holiness; he is the model of
prelates who are committed to the Church and to her sons, as

Bernard remarked in Letter 50 to Pope Honorius III; he offers an example of life to monks, as explained in the 51st of his assorted sermons: he suffered labors and persecutions for love of Jesus.

This mystery of holiness all the members of the Church should realize, each for himself, since it is a matter of personal union with God, but also as a whole, since the Church is a community, a *congregatio*, a communion with Christ in the Spirit whom he has sent. Certainly Bernard was well aware that there were believers in name only, *vel nomine tenus fide*, and he even said that "few men are saved". But he did not exclude from the Church those who remain united to her

> ...either by the sacraments which they receive
> indiscriminately along with those who lead a good
> life, or because of the common faith which they
> profess, or at least by reason of the fact that they
> live in the corporal society of the faithful, or by
> hope of salvation to come—which such men should
> never despair of in this life, even if they live lives
> of desperation.   (*On the Song of Songs* 25, 2)

This allusion to the benefits of living in community, in the "corporal society", reminds us of the high esteem which the abbot of Clairvaux had for the brotherly life of the monks. More than once he spoke of the "grace of a common life", *socialis vitae gratia* (*Sermon for the Vigil of Christmas* 5, 6), the "sweetness of the grace of community", *suavitas gratiae socialis* (*On the Song of Songs* 44, 5). Elsewhere he showed the value that other's faith can have in supporting our own. Referring to the mysteries of Jesus' infancy, Bernard wrote:

> How could the human race, the entire earthly
> globe be convinced of such a thing? And yet this
> persuasion was accomplished so easily and so
> profoundly that such a belief is now made easy for
> me by the multitude of believers. (*Sermon for the
> Vigil of Christmas* 3, 9)

Because it is a society as well as a mystery, the Church has legislation and a hierarchy. Toward canon law, Bernard displayed a certain casualness. Toward the end of the treatise *On Precept and Dispensation* (n. 57), he wrote: *"Talia nostra non refert, qui monachi sumus*; this has little relevance for us who are monks." But he did not preach this monastic attitude for everyone. Without being a specialist in ecclesiastical law, he was familiar with it and occasionally referred to it, though not very often. His conduct at the time of the schism of Anacletus, the manner in which he viewed relationship between ecclesiastical and civil powers over episcopal elections, several scattered quotations in his works, several manuscripts known to have been in his possession: all of these factors support the contention that he had read the *Panormia*, a collection of texts gathered together by Bishop Yves of Chartres, and that he was inspired by the moderate views of this particular prelate. He maintained too the principle of the pope's universal authority. We have seen how he himself had occasion to turn to this authority—for example, when Abelard was on trial. But like Yves, he reacted against the excessive centralization of pontifical powers. In particular, he protested against the exhorbitant amount of power accorded to legates, against the requests of some monasteries for exemption from local diocesan authority, against the frequency of "appeals" which drove some to recourse to Rome in opposition to the bishops. With regard to the Roman Curia, he posed this question: "Why not choose from among all of the people those who will one day judge all of the people?" At a time when the prerogatives of the cardinals were increasing and the pageantry of the pontifical court was growing more ostentatious, Bernard, faithful to the Cistercian spirit and to the real demands of the reform, insisted on poverty and simplicity, on an evangelical conception of the government of the Church. His tracts *On the Duties and Conduct of Bishops* and *On Consideration* contain many forceful and courageous pages on the hierarchy of service.

Finally the Church, because it is a society of sanctification, includes the just who have preceded us before God. Influenced by texts from St Augustine and St Ambrose which had been forgotten, Bernard elaborated a theory on the subject of the elect, especially in the *Sermons for All Saints Day* and in his treatise *On the Love of God.* It was a strange theory, but one which deserves to be recalled briefly because it concludes and clarifies his synthesis of the supernatural world. According to Bernard, the elect are already in heaven, in the light, with Christ. But before the resurrection, souls separated from their bodies do not yet have a place in the "house of God": they await in the outer sanctuary—the *tabernacula* often spoken of in the Bible—the day when they can be completely blessed. They are already at rest, but not in beatitude. They are definitively united to God, but not perfectly. This will be accomplished when the reunited body and soul both participate in the Resurrection of Christ and the integrity of his Body which is the Church.

> It is not fitting that complete beatitude be granted
> before the one who will receive it is a complete
> man; no more than perfection can be bestowed on
> a still imperfect Church. (*For All Saints Day* 3, 1)

Thus, between the provisional "tents" where the militant Church sets up camp and the "dwelling place" of the risen Church, there is a place for a waiting period. Bernard's point of view was never confirmed by the *magisterium* of the Church, but at least it evinces of the high esteem which he had for the body.

It also demonstrates the importance, in his experience and in his teaching, of the desire for God. He often speaks of this "thirst", this "eagerness", this completely spiritual "concupiscence", this "tension toward the infinite", this "strong desire to see God", to possess him completely and to be wholly with him. Death, which he viewed with serenity, will be the passage from the provisional to the eternal: "At last, to see forever him who has been forever sought." The waiting period is also a time of gratitude: Bernard likewise often insisted on thanksgiving. He thanked the Lord for gifts already received: grace, conversion, a life of communion in the cloister and in the Church, the promise of eternal life. He gave thanks to the Virgin and the saints for the help given us by their examples and their intercession. He gave thanks to men, each of whom, in his own milieu and according to his own function, serves the others and supports them, ever draws them on, by his prayer and his desire. For there are many gifts but only one Spirit, many rooms but only one house. In a manuscript from Citeaux, the Church, City of God, is represented by an embattled tower where three characters appear: the one in the center, dressed in purple, represents the priesthood which wields the sword of the Word of God; on the right, a soldier carries the temporal sword and; on the other side, a monk, weeping from repentance and joy, symbolizes all those who have no other weapons but prayer and charity.

BERNARD'S LATER IMAGE AND INFLUENCE

His Contemporaries

WHEN BERNARD DIED AT CLAIRVAUX on the morning of 20 August 1153, the future of his work was assured as well as threatened by posterity. The spirit of Bernard lives on in his sons. But they are so numerous and so scattered that it would prove difficult for them, as for the entire Cistercian Order, to preserve the very exacting ideal of the man who had animated with his own fervor this body which had grown too quickly and become too extensive. A map of the "claravallian world" at the time of Bernard's death shows rays emanating, as from a luminous hearth, from the abbey which he had governed, and reaching out in some cases almost a thousand miles—at that time, an enormous distance. There were one hundred and sixty-seven monasteries distributed throughout Ireland, England, Sweden, Germany, southern Italy, Sardinia, Spain, and Portugal. Seventy-one of these "daughters, grand-daughters, and great granddaughters" of Clairvaux were located in France, forty-one in England. Some of these monasteries numbered as many as seven hundred inhabitants. Following the death of such a line's ancestor, enthusiasm would diminish. In one century, Clairvaux founded no more than a dozen houses. Most of all, the spirit would be weakened. The Order of Cîteaux continued to develop and to extend itself into new lands, but, from the last months of the very year of Bernard's death, in his monastery as in the general chapter of the

Order, actions were taken which weakened the principle of an economy assured mainly by the work of monks, and to the program of poverty which St Bernard had done everything in his power to preserve.

Fortunately, his writings maintained his presence everywhere. During his lifetime, copies of his works had been distributed among his foundations and in all of the daughter houses throughout his own Order, in Benedictine monasteries, among the Canons Regular, the Premonstratensians, the Carthusians, and in the cathedrals. A chart indicating the diffusion of bernardine manuscripts during the twelfth century proves that these had penetrated well beyond the "claravallian world" itself, especially in central Europe and as far as the center of Poland. The Rhineland, Bavaria, and Austria possessed large numbers of these texts, as did Normandy, northern France, and Belgium. These facts are partially explained by Bernard's travels, by his activity at the time of the Crusade, and by his distant family ancestry: according to his geneology, he was related to a number of noblemen and prelates, many of whom lived between the Rhine and the Seine and who had offered him land for his foundations and had given him occasion to intervene in these areas. More than 1,500 manuscripts of Bernard's works have survived all threats of disappearance, and nearly half of these date from his own time. This high figure seems to constitute a unique case in literary history.

A curious fact is that the copies drawn up at Clairvaux are not among his best. On the one hand, he had to work in haste in order to answer requests which came from all of his daughter houses and from admirers everywhere. The writings were transcribed without the necessary care and corrected in the same way, sometimes with new errors added to the original. On the other hand, from the day of Bernard's death, there was an movement to request his canonization. To obtain this more easily, some individuals assumed the right to modify his texts, with the intention of improving them. A group of grammar experts, who lacked nothing but literary genius, set to work on this project. Some, moreover, wished to eliminate certain passages erroneously considered dangerous to his "reputation of sanctity", such as that passage in Letter 70 where he had admitted feelings of anger. In a word, his writing suffered from these manipulations and came out weakened and mangled. The "milieu" had taken action in a way comparable to what the Visitation of Annecy would later do to the writings of Francis de Sales, Port-Royal to those of Paschal, and the Carmel of Lisieux to those of St Thérèse of the Child Jesus. Today, the best witnesses to an exact text from St Bernard are found as far as possible from Clairvaux, in England or in Austria.

Bernard lived on in his readers and it happened that he was admired more and more as a writer than as man of action or an abbot. Certainly in his own milieu delightful memories of him were preserved. Those who had seen or heard him, and especially those who had lived and worked with him, could not forget his personal charm. In the funeral oration which he wrote eight days after having assisted at Bernard's death, Odo of Morimund expressed the emotion of all. More than once, Geoffrey of Auxerre, his secretary and successor, referred to his "humanity". The lay brother Lawrence, the confidential clerk who had so often distributed Bernard's correspondence throughout the Church, was deeply distressed. It was soon retold that he had complained in a prayer beside the body of his deceased abbot:

> While you were alive, it often happened that I traveled great distances, by your orders, and I left with confidence and transmitted your reports and your letters...

Then Bernard had appeared to him and promised that he would continue to help him. In fact, the first time that Lawrence had to make a return trip to Rome, he was received everywhere as an object of such concern and generosity, in memory of his abbot, that he brought back five pair of buffalo. He had only the help of two children crossing the Alps, "and each of these beasts was greater in size than two or three ordinary bulls." Such was the man called Bernard, "whose face the whole world longed to see", as the biographer of Blessed Giraud de Sales would later write. Many, including bishops, wished to spend their last days either as guests or as monks in the place where he had died; the expression "to die at Clairvaux" became proverbial.

It is understandable that, in his monastery as well as in many other places, there was a great desire to have his sanctity recognized and proclaimed by the Holy See. Geoffrey of Auxerre was commissioned to complete the "Life" which had been begun by William of Saint Thierry and Arnaud de Bonneval. He revised their work and added his own, and the first draft of the whole text was submitted to the judgment of a group of abbots. After that, a second edition was drawn up wherein certain portions which might cast a bad light on contemporaries who were still living were toned down or eliminated altogether. The complete text was finished in 1165. Since 1159, which was only six years after his death, Bernard's liturgical commemoration had been authorized at Clairvaux. In 1162, the monks from this monastery requested that Alexander III canonize him, and twelve years later, in 1174, the bull of canonization was promulgated, after which the body of the saint was "raised", that is placed above an altar, and his cult became widespread. His name was given to children, and the texts of the Missal which celebrated his praises spoke of him as a doctor of the Church.

In fact, many panegyrics exalted his doctrine. Not that all of his teachings and examples were approved. In particular, the canonists of the second half of the twelfth century were cautious with regard to his ideas on the exercise of pontifical power. They tended to accord greater importance to juridical structures than he had. Likewise, the letter to the Canons of Lyon on the feast of the conception of the Virgin Mary continued to provoke contrary reactions. For his part, the Cistercian Evrard of Ypres was quick to point out that he and others held the thought of Gilbert of Poitiers in greater esteem than that of Bernard when it pertained to certain chapters of theology. Nevertheless, many teachers and

writers declared their admiration. John of Salisbury said that
the Holy Spirit had spoken by the mouth of Bernard. Guerric
of Igny had already referred to him as "interpreter for the
Holy Spirit". Otto of Freising praised "his wisdom and his
literary ability." John of Ford considered him a "giant"
because of "the spirit of charity which he had experienced
and communicated." Isaac of Stella, while having reser-
vations on certain points, acknowledged the intense spiritual
joy which flowed from his work. Clarembald of Arras
referred to "the abbot Bernard, of happy memory." Gerhoch
of Reichersberg, Peter of Celle, Thomas of Perseigne, and
several anonymous transcribers expressed themselves with
the same measure of enthusiasm, considering him equal in
stature to Origen and Gregory the Great.

Less than ten years after Bernard's death, an abbot from
the Benedictine monastery of Anchin began a collection of his
writings and of the hagiographical accounts concerning him.
The first complete edition, finished in 1165 and beautifully
illustrated, is still preserved in three great volumes at the
Library of Douai (ms 372). Nicholas of Clairvaux, who had at
one time been Bernard's secretary but had had to be
dismissed because he had made bad use of Bernard's seal,
before 1159 and at the request of Pope Adrian IV, composed
a collection of sermons, "not as the abbot of Clairvaux had
delivered them", but as he himself, Nicholas, had written
them. Geoffrey of Auxerre set down in writing the preaching
which Bernard had addressed to the clergy of Cologne, and
several anonymous disciples composed sermons in St
Bernard's style, drawing inspiration from his teachings or
attempting to remember what he had said some twenty years
before. As for his masterpiece, the series of *Sermons on the
Song of Songs*, it was the continual subject of commentaries,
summaries in prose and verse, and of a whole *genre* of
literature. Toward the end of the twelfth century, this work
as well as the great liturgical sermons was being translated
into French. It was an acknowledged fact that all of these
texts were difficult reading, requiring not only attentive study
but a certain affinity with the soul of their author. A

transcriber would one day apply to Bernard the words that
William of Saint Thierry had spoken with regard to St Paul:

> No one can understand the words of St Bernard if
> he has not acquired, according to his own capacity,
> the meaning of St Bernard. (*The Golden Epistle*
> *I:121*)

His reputation inspired poets who composed epitaphs and
eulogies of all sorts in his honor or pursued bizarre
etymologies of his name with the intention of relating it to the
Sacred Scriptures which he loved so well. By their interpretation "Ber" is derived from the Hebrew meaning of source,
and "nard" was that hidden but sweet-smelling plant, a
symbol of humility in fervor, which is mentioned in the *Song
of Songs*. At the same time, the title of *Mellifluus* was
beginning to be applied to him. This term had a precise significance in the medieval exegetical tradition. It was
composed of two words, the first referring to honey and the
second to the act of flowing: the "mellifluous one" is the
one who draws the spiritual meaning from the letter of the
Bible, and Bernard had excelled in this manner of interpretation. In the area of iconography, the dominant traits of
Bernard's image were fixed: he was often represented in the
act of writing, or holding in his hands the book of Sacred
Scriptures, displaying the Bible before commenting on it and
initiating "the flow" of mystical doctrine.

And already certain writings were being attributed to St
Bernard which were not his. This was particularly true with
several works by his biographers, William of Saint Thierry
and Arnaud of Bonneval, then Drogo of Laon and other black
monks, many Cistercian authors, several Canons Regular, and
finally some anonymous authors who have not yet been
identified, but whose work, of genuine quality, such as the
"Meditations on the Understanding of the Human Condition"
and an admirable hymn on the name of Jesus which begins
"Jesu dulcis memoria", was widely diffused. Thus Bernard's
patronage covers writings which were inspired by his own but
which are often inferior to his. His name assures their

success. His legend continued to develop. Toward the year
1178, Herbert, a monk from Clairvaux who had become Archbishop of Sardinia, composed a "Book of the Miracles of St
Bernard" where he demonstrates greater admiration and
imagination than critical judgment. The same credulity and
the same fervor is also evident in the "Second Life" written
by Alan of Auxerre in about 1170; in the "Third Life", a
work by John the Hermit in about 1180; then in the "Great
Beginnings of the Order of Cîteaux" from the pen of Conrad
of Eberbach; and in the "Dialogues" of Caesarius of
Heisterbach.

What kind of image did Bernard leave behind him, which
his contemporaries transmitted to succeeding generations up
to the end of the twelfth century? It had both been enriched
by legendary elements—which only happens to men who are
truly great—and simplified. Many of the concrete circumstances had been forgotten, but the striking features of his
personality were retained. What are these? In the first
place, Bernard appears as a mystic, a man of prayer, one who
has enjoyed the experience of union with God. We come to
his school in order to learn how to imitate him in this area. A
copyist from the abbey of Salem said of him: "He had
received a special gift for meditation," adding that, if he was
an excellent "meditator", it was because he had first been an
ardent "reader" of Sacred Scripture. He could comment on
it because he had assimilated it: he merits our esteem as a
spiritual interpreter of the word of God, and his eloquence
was but an overflow of his own intimate devotion. As
exacting a scholar as John of Salisbury did not stint his
praises for Bernard's talents as an orator:

> When he was given the opportunity to express
> himself, he nearly succeeded in persuading all to
> his way of thinking.... He was such a remarkable
> preacher that, after St Gregory, I do not think that
> anyone can be compared to him. His style was
> particularly elegant....

And Wiebald of Stavelot, who had heard him speak,

described him in this way:

> His body, emaciated by the fasts and austerities of
> the desert, and his pallor give him a quasi-
> spiritualized aspect: the mere appearance of this
> man convinces his listeners even before he opens
> his mouth.... His gestures were always appro-
> priate.... Just to see such a man is an instruction
> in itself....

The Age of The Schools

During the thirteenth century, the golden age of Scholasticism, when so many teachers would express themselves,
when distinguished scholars would provoke such progress in
theology, were the teachings of St Bernard forgotten? Certainly the Abbot of Clairvaux was no longer one of the great
names in the science of religion, but he remained present,
active and fertile. Already during the great upsurge of
thought which characterized the second half and the end of
the twelfth century, there had been recourse to him. Some of
his texts had been used in the *Sentences* of Peter Lombard
and were destined to exercise a limited but very precise
influence. Many writers, especially some of those in the
school of Saint Victor, and the authors of anonymous *Summas*
quoted passages from his treatise *On Grace and Free Will*;
and Phillip, Chancellor of the University of Paris at the
beginning of the thirteenth century, made great use of this
book and contributed to the spread of its ideas. The Franciscans became particularly sensitive to it: several among
them referred to the treatise and the Masters, Alexander of
Hales and Bonaventure, and their disciples at the end of the
century frequently appealed to the work of St Bernard. On
the other hand, the Dominicans do not accord him a
prominent place, at least in their doctrine, but they were not
lacking in devotion toward him. St Thomas Aquinas left a
sermon for his feast and it was later recounted that, before
his death at the Cistercian Abbey of Fossanova where had
had been invited by the monks to comment on the *Song of
Songs* "as St Bernard used to do", he had said: "Grant me

the spirit of St Bernard and I will reproduce his commentary.''

In fact, with Bernard and Thomas, we find two orientations of religious thought which were to complement each other, which many had once been able to reconcile, but which would soon become very distinct before separating altogether.   In that theology was becoming not only speculative but abstract, and that it was borrowing Aristotle's method, those who had merely engaged in commenting on the Bible seemed capable of nurturing piety but not theological thought.   Several devotional tracts, written chiefly by Franciscans, were circulated under St Bernard's name, and from his own works the Benedictine William of Toumai managed to extract a large collection of choice pieces, ''Flores'', which were destined to be copied and edited many times over.   Mingled with the authentic texts were apocryphal pages from different pseudo-Bernards which had already become quite numerous. The treatise *On Precept and Dispensation* was frequently added to the Rule of St Benedict by way of commentary. Matthew, a subcantor at Rievaulx, and others composed poems in Bernard's honor; and Helinand of Froidmond, the gay troubadour turned Cistercian, not content with having sung his praises in a ''Chronicle'', had dedicated to Bernard several stanzas of his ''Lines on Death'', so human, so discreet in their emotion:

> Death, death, greet Bernard in my name,
> My companion, now in God's special care,
> For whom my heart sighs and weeps....

The golden age of Scholasticism was also a great century of rhetoric.   Bernard's literary talent was admired.   An anonymous Cistercian, speaking of his ''elegant elocution'', characterized him as a new Anthony of monks, and, among orators, a new Cicero: *monachorum Antonius et Tullius oratorum.*   In books on the ''Art of Preaching'', his sermons were referred to as models and his methods carefully analysed; for, Robert of Basevorn stated, everything in him is artistic, the composition as well as the style.

Finally, it was during the thirteenth century that the "marian legend of St Bernard" assumed its final shape. It includes two aspects, both regrettable. For one, Nicholas of Saint Alban, an English Benedictine and a notable though somewhat bitter theologian had, since the second half of the preceding century, related a dream attributed to a lay brother from Cîteaux: St Bernard had supposedly appeared to him, all dressed in white save for a stain on his breast, and had explained that this was "a mark of the purification which he had to suffer because of what he had written concerning the conception of Our Lady." This spiteful legend, which was not at all justified—the letter to the Canons of Lyon was all ot the glory of the Virgin Mary—was then widely publicized and commented on, approved by some and rejected by others. And it was no doubt as a means of attack against this legend that others felt obliged to exaggerate the praises accorded Bernard's marian doctrine and to fabricate other accounts of "miracles" where the Mother of God showed special favor toward him. The authors of anthologies or works of piety acted in the same vein, drawing much of their inspiration from texts which had been falsely attributed to the abbot of Clairvaux. Iconography represented this confused situation. The oldest marian image of St Bernard depicts him admonishing a group of clerics; it could be assumed that they were the Canons of Lyon, since the picture is found in the ornate initial at the beginning of the letter addressed to them. Others represent him in tears at the feet of the Virgin, at the beginning of the "Complaint" of Ogier de Locedio. Or again, at the start of a piece by Arnold of Bonneval, he is seen contemplating Christ who displays his wounds before the Father while Mary, in a gesture inspired by that of Hecubus in the *Iliad*, offers her breast to her Son. Henceforth, based on faith in the apocryphal writings, Bernard would appear to have written a great deal on the subject of the Mother of God.

Centuries of Crisis

At the beginning of the following period, two writers and

two of the founding fathers of that literary humanism which would react against the extreme dialectical character of scholasticism accorded a privileged place to St Bernard in their work and in their esteem. First Dante, a victim of that "marian legend" which he helped to reinforce, chose St Bernard, an "old man clothed in glory", to introduce him in the *Paradiso* to the Queen who is full of grace. And from the mouth of Bernard comes one of the most beautiful prayers to Our Lady that has ever been written:

> Virgin Mother, daughter of your Son,
> More humble and greater than any creature...

In his treatise on the universal government of the world, *De monarchia,* where he withdrew all power from the pope and attributed it to the emperor, Dante made much of the pages from *On Consideration* which sought to reduce the temporal authority of the Roman Pontiff. Here again it was a partial use of the texts, and he drew more from them than they in fact contained. But his intentions were just when he replaced Beatrice with the abbot of Clairvaux at the moment when the flight toward God is to be consummated: for Bernard is the theologian of union with God, "this man of contemplation who freely—that is, rightfully—assumes the function of scholar." For his part, Petrarch would go on from there to praise the inspired character of Bernard's style and teachings, saying that he had learned everything not from men and books but from the oak and beech trees while he prayed and meditated in the forest, in the sylvan wilderness.

Even before Dante's time, Bernard's name had been called upon in the doctrinal polemics occasioned by the conflicts arising between princes and popes. At the time of the dispute between Boniface VIII and Phillip the Fair, as well as in similar quarrels with emperors and kings, Bernard was invoked by those who held opposing political theories. His works could support pontifical authority, but they also sought to set restrictions on it. John Wycliff used ideas from *On Consideration* which supported his theses: he isolated from their context all the criticisms directed against the ostentation and abuses of the Roman Curia and turned them into arguments against the papacy itself. What Bernard wished to reform, he hoped to destroy. Thereafter, Bernard was constantly quoted by the adversaries of the Church and the hierarchy. In the Church itself, however, his constructive work continued: *On Consideration* was represented nowhere as abundantly as in the Vatican Library. Many popes and cardinals wanted to possess a copy of this treatise, to read it for inspiration, and even to have it illuminated in such luxurious style as would have offended the author. During the worst periods of Roman decadence, this text remained a witness to the ideal and those who summarized it in statements destined for the highest prelates used it as a program of reform.

In the area of theology, John XXII, an Avignon Pope, as a private scholar, had revived Bernard's opinion on the incomplete beatitude of the saints before the resurrection of their bodies. His successor, Benedict XII—paradoxically a Cistercian—rejected these ideas and reaffirmed the common faith. In 1379, Henry of Langenstein, a professor in Paris, published a work entitled "Against the Stain which was Falsely Imposed on St Bernard". If the legend of the stain was tenacious, the marian legend was no less so and it was continually enriched by new themes: there was the story of the "lactation", according to which the Virgin had squeezed her breast and directed the flow of milk toward St Bernard. The theme was developed with many variations and represented in many different fashions, some of which were not in the best taste. Often the abbot of Clairvaux was depicted weeping at the foot of the Cross. The theologian, the contemplative scholar so admired by Dante, appeared as a pious author. Never were there so many pseudo-Bernards, never were so many apocryphal writings composed and translated in his name, as during the period of the "Devotio Moderna". It was at this time that the cliché arose associating Bernard with a sensible devotion to the humanity of Christ. Then too the meaning of the title "Mellifluous" was altered: it became synonymous with meekness, a "flowing sweetness".   Texts which are not even his transformed the mystic into a sentimentalist.   His own writings were difficult, profound in a way which was no longer understood, drawn from biblical inspiration whose meaning had long since been lost.   Nevertheless, the fresco which Fra Angelico would paint on a wall at San Marco would still represent him as a contemplative gazing with serenity on the mystery of God and holding the Bible in his hands.

With the widespread use of printing, the authentic works of St Bernard experienced a revival.   Incunabulum editions appeared, some partial and confused.   But from the beginning of the sixteenth century critical endeavors became manifest.   Collections of his complete works were published and it was maintained that the text had been verified according to copies from Clairvaux.   This phrase was little more than a stereotype, but it does express a concern for proper research: an attempt was at least made to collect all of his writings.   Bernard's works were reprinted more often than any of the other Church Fathers':   even St Augustine did not have such good fortune.   If the great scholarly humanists of the time could perceive the worth of Bernard's work and preferred it to that of the Scholastics, it is because of its fullness both of doctrine and of beauty.   Ideas and phrases were drawn from it on all sides.   Luther found words and pages which he took out of context and used as arguments to support his own views on the christian condition or on the authority of the Church.   He was also sensitive to the intense religious value of the spiritual experience which Bernard analyzes and renders so desirable.   By this very fact, Luther stands at the origins of a whole Bernardine tradition in protestantism, to which we owe a long series of German translations.   The reformers working within the bosom of the Catholic Church, also made use of Bernard's ideas, his fervor, and his beauty.   Polanco, secretary to St Ignatius of Loyola, wishing to offer to the Society of Jesus some examples of letters to be written, suggested that they read those of the abbot of Clairvaux.

The Baroque Period

The seventeenth and eighteenth centuries for those European countries which had remained Catholic were a time of exuberant vitality that manifested itself in what is called the baroque culture, which was extended in the rococo style of art. There was also a baroque and rococo St Bernard. All that the preceding period had created in the way of apocrypha and legends was now printed, translated, commented on, and illustrated. In this area, masterpieces of engraving, painting and sculpture were produced: it is enough to mention the "Lactations" and other tableaux by Murillo, Ribera, and many great names of the time. But all of these belated themes, inherited from recent centuries, could only serve to enhance in the eyes of the general public a false idea of St Bernard. To the title "Mellifluus", with its very affected intepretation, was added that of "Nectarifluus". Collections of excerpts partially inauthentic, were published whose titles gave prominence to the notion of honey: "Melliloquium, Mellilegium, Sweet drops from the Words of Honey, Mystic Bee or Sweet-Smelling Florets of Honeyed Discourses, Marian Bee, Claravallian Bee-hive." Bavaria and the Austro-Hungarian countries, a paradise of baroque, set the tone. But in France also, Camus, the Bishop of Belley, praised Bernard for his "discourses more loveable than love itself, sweeter than honey itself." In Portugal, the "theme of Jesus Crucified" gave rise to tender and beautiful effusions, but owed nothing to St Bernard even though it lay claim to him as its authority.

In this same country, all kinds of documents were being forged—several of which were letters attributed to Bernard and which have since become part of every edition—to establish the fact that, during the twelfth century, the abbot of Clairvaux had been in touch with the first King of Portugal, Alfonso Henriques, through the intermediary of his brother Peter, whom we know today never existed. Elsewhere the Gallicans, Josephinists, and other opponents of papal intervention in the religious politics of the kingdoms

and the Empire continued to turn to *On Consideration* for
their arguments. In Spain, two Jesuit theologians, Salmeron
and Suarez, in the elaboration of their marian doctrine, drew
intelligent inspiration from Bernard's authentic texts whose
biblical depth they fully recognized.

In France, the centuries of baroque were a classical age.
Not that the fervor and imagination never led to extremes.
But the most generous knew how to keep the measure. Rancé
himself, who could be so excessive at times, referred to St
Bernard as: "This man who was so moderate and so just in
his feelings." As in monastic controversies, Bernard was
invoked by both sides in the quarrel with Jansenism and in
the dispute between Fenelon and Bossuet. Berulle and the
spiritualists of the French school who laid such stress on consideration of the mysteries of the Incarnate Word revealed
notable affinities with some of Bernard's teachings. The
Benedictines of the Congregation of Saint Maur at Saint
Germain des Prés did not fail to pay tribute to the abbot of
Clairvaux in their scholarly work. The time had indeed come
to exert critical skill in unravelling the confusion of texts
which were circulating under the name of St Bernard.
Mabillon was the main author of this venture. Stimulated by
Dom Luke of Achery, he consulted the learned men of the
time (Bona in Rome, others in Flanders and elsewhere),
examined and collated the manuscripts, and thus prepared a
complete edition which was printed for the first time in 1667.
The judgments concerning authenticity are altogether definitive. And yet this scholar, rightly called illustrious, had the
humility—which in this case was actually a weakness–to side
with Rancé's opinion when he tried to persuade him that the
last part of Letter 70, where Bernard told of his anger with
his brother Bartholomew, could *a priori* not be authentic
because it was so contrary to all that was known about the
holiness of this great abbot. Mabillon, who had formerly
admitted that "saints occasionally have minor outbursts, of
which they later disapprove," thus rejected, in a footnote to
the second edition, this text which had already suffered at the

hands of proofreaders at Clairvaux during the years preparatory to Bernard's canonization, when manuscripts from the mother abbey were eliminated. At least Mabillon had elsewhere praised the "strength and vitality" of Bernard's style: *vim et energiam.* The phrase can also be applied to his teaching and his personality: by way of compensation for the abuses of the term "mellifluous", Père Raynaud, a contemporary Jesuit, compared St Bernard to a "bellicose bee."

Finally Pascal, one of the greatest religious figures of this great French age, agreed with the abbot of Clairvaux on more than one point. Let us not forget that Port Royal had once been a Cistercian monastery. But Pascal learned something other than ideas on grace or encouragements toward austerity from Bernard: a sense of the absoluteness of God's demands, the necessity of love to awaken this understanding, the consent which can only be given to the "heart" by the Spirit. And his "You would not seek me if you had not already found me" is drawn word for word from the treatise *On the Love of God.*

During the eighteenth century, St Bernard's works were reedited with a more accurate knowledge of their authenticity. Nevertheless, legends built up before Mabillon's time continued to hold fast in devout milieux and to furnish themes for iconography. At the time of the French Revolution, some of the more violent Republicans stormed Bernard's tomb. But the people who lived in the neighborhood of Clairvaux demanded that the body be restored. It was broken up into relics and, in 1813, the skull was transferred, along with that of St Malachy, to the Cathedral of Troyes where it is still venerated today.

Modern Times

In the first half of the nineteenth century, during the wave of Romanticism, Bernard became for Catholic apologetics a kind of symbol of what the power of the spirit had been in the centuries of christianity. The idealized and simplistic image that has been formed of the Middle Ages permitted a projection into this little known past of the regrets which had given rise to recent ruptures. At the age of twenty-five, toward the year 1835, the young Count of Montalembert dreamt of writing a "Life of St Bernard". He wrote the Introduction, which would not be published despite the entreaties of Dom Gueranger because, on the advice of Monsignor Dupanloup, the author had decided to improve and develop it: it would become a large book in several volumes entitled *The Monks of the West*. But the saint whose biography was prevented by the larger work and certain political struggles remains present throughout these volumes. And we can catch an echo of that grandiloquence which was popular at the time in this statement on St Bernard:

> No one has cast as much splendor as he on the garb of the monk. By universal consent, he was a man of genius: he influenced his own century in an unprecedented manner; he ruled by his eloquence, his virtue, and his courage. More than once, he decided the fate of peoples and of crowns; once he even held the destiny of the Church in his hands. He knew how to arouse all of Europe and fling her toward the Orient; he fought and conquered, in the person of Abelard, the precursor of modern rationalism. The whole world knows and acknowledges this: everyone willingly ranks him alongside Ximenes, Richelieu, and Bossuet. But that is not enough... .

Montelembert's allusion to Abelard shows how the apologetics of romanticism contributed to the popularization of a cliché which was not its own invention: the defeat of rationalism. The opponents of this same apologetics used this legend against Bernard: Abelard became the symbol of free thinking oppressed by the obscurantism of the Church. His works were published, his correspondence translated, and the editions dating from this period, illustrated in sentimental taste, with a grandiloquence that was not totally lacking in

charm, offer the picture of a poor intellectual dominated by a
hard and authoritarian abbot.   It is true that, in pious
milieux, the theme of bees and honey had begun to enhance
the term mellifluous, and was occasionally combined with the
notion of "lactation" in an iconography so bizarre and com-
plicated as to be equivalent with bad taste.   Never, with
regard to St Bernard, had matters reached such a low point.

It was not until the end of the nineteenth century that a
reaction set in.   The year 1891 was the 800th anniversary of
Bernard's birth.   P. Janauschek, an Austrian Cistercian,
published a vast "Bernardine Bibliography" which cata-
logued the 2,761 works which had appeared on the subject of
the abbot of Clairvaux since the invention of the printing
press.   A statue was raised in a plaza at Dijon which received
the name of St Bernard, "orator and statesman".   Another
event, which was interior but destined to have important re-
percussions, happened to Maurice Blondel who was then a
student.   Let us listen as he speaks for himself:

> A citizen of Dijon, I watched the preparations
> underway for the great celebrations in honor of the
> eighth centenary of St Bernard's birth, and for me
> it was an occasion to read a large part of the
> writings of this Great Doctor, this great mystic,
> this great man of action who, before the technical
> systematizations of the thirteenth and fourteenth
> centuries, drew directly from the living sources of
> tradition, as well as from his own personal
> ascetical and mystical experience.

Harnack declared that in the writings of St Bernard could be
found "the religious genius of the twelfth century".   In 1895,
Abbot Vacandard published a "Life of St Bernard" in two
volumes which remains a monument of honest erudition and
intelligence.

However, if Bernard held a place in the works of historians
and in devotional literature and in the philosophical thinking
of Blondel and his disciples, he had not yet been taken
seriously by the theologians.   It would be the task of Etienne

Gilson to bring him to their attention in a book where he published the lessons given by him at the College of France. Its very title suggests a complete program and almost a manifesto: *The Mystical Theology of Saint Bernard.* First published in 1934, this book is still the most beautiful one written on the abbot of Clairvaux. A number of his expressions have become classics, particularly the one where he calls Bernard a "theologian whose powers of synthesis and speculative abilities rank him among the greatest names." But for many among art historians as well as in ecclesiastical circles, Bernard was still merely a "pious author", even though a scholar like Dom Wilmart had protested against the false ideas that were retained on the subject of his "devotion to the humanity of Christ" and his mariology, which was nearly transformed into a "mariolatry". Nevertheless, in 1944, there appeared in Algeria the secret but admirable translation of *Consideration* by Pierre Dalloz entitled "Counsels to the Pope", but whose intention was to offer to other rulers these counsels of courage.

1953 was the year of the eighth centenary of Bernard's death. A wave of publications spoke of him in Europe and around the world, ceremonies took place, congresses were celebrated whose actions have been preserved in several useful volumes. The two main results of this contribution made to Bernardine studies by famous medievalists were: better to situate and, consequently, restrict St Bernard's active role in the history of his time; and to reveal the specific nature of his teachings. His work and his thought had until then been treated like those Roman churches of the baroque period, laden with adventitious ornaments which tended to engross the attention. It was now a matter of rediscovering this "Roman theology" which had preceded and to a certain extent prepared the way for the cathedrals of the golden age of Gothic and Scholasticism. Bernard emerged from this vast cleaning process as more real, and certainly no less great. The volume *Saint Bernard, Théologien*, an effort in which a whole series of eminent researchers collaborated, gave new impetus to studies in this area. Ever since the centenary

these studies have continued. They reveal ever more clearly
the actual role played by Bernard in the doctrinal develop-
ments of his time and the traditional character of his
teachings.   Much more than the witness to a "new
sensitivity", he appears as the distinguished, though not
unique, representative of the mentality of the Church Fathers
which was still living in the twelfth century; in a word, he is
the symbol of what has been called "medieval patristics."

A new "Bernardine Bibliography" covering the years up to
1957 enumerated more than one thousand publications
relating to St Bernard which had appeared in sixty years'
time. A complete and critical edition of his works has been
undertaken, most volumes of which have already appeared. It
will not be flawless, and some feel that its main worth lies
in the opportunity offered for studies of the history and
quality of the text and of the author's literary personality. In
Eastern Europe, the hundred year old myth is being revived
and clothed in socio-economic terms which show Bernard
oppressing the free thought of Abelard, stifling a revolution
with the help of reactionary powers, wealth, and the
aristocracy.   But researchers everywhere still admire the
value of his style, probe his theological ideas, study his
exegesis and his sources, uncovering the biblical and
liturgical substratum which has made it so fruitful.   From
time to time, a Cistercian pen will erroneously attribute to
him some words which he never wrote and would indeed have
taken exception to: *"De Maria numquam satis:*   one can
never say enough about the Virgin Mary."   Meanwhile a new
mode of progress in penetration and precision is being
ushered in by historians who review Bernard's texts in the
light of more recent theses and hypotheses, such as those of
Freud.   A whole current of christian existentialism
acknowledges a certain closeness to Bernard: Lavelle, Forest,
Jankelevitch, and others have quoted him. In another area of
spiritual movement during our own times, John XXIII
referred to him and, in his *Journal of a Soul* confided:

During my meals, I have several pages of St

Bernard's *De Consideratione* read to me... Nothing is better adapted and more useful for a poor pope such as I am, and for a pope at any time. Something of the dishonor that marked the Roman clergy in the twelfth century is always with us. We must be vigilant, make amends, and persevere.

Paul VI mentioned St Bernard several months after his elevation to the office of Supreme Pontiff, in the great discourse of 21 September 1963 where he announced the reform of the Curia. This inspired the following commentary by Père Rouquette:

De Consideratione proposes to a pope of the twelfth century a positive and very real program of service, simplicity, poverty in the apostolic spirit, abdication of any notions of domination or tyranny, and religious purity of intention. Paul VI meditates on *De Consideratione* and draws inspiration from it. Eugene III could hardly put into effect St Bernard's program, and his reign was the prelude of a rise in temporal power under Innocent III at the end of the same century. It is not impossible to conceive that Paul VI may well be the Pope envisioned by the Abbot of Clairvaux.

The Real St Bernard

He will be read more and more in translations. Accustomed to the Latin and rhetorical forms, the ancients were more sensitive to his literary talents than we are. Yet, even in those languages where much of the biblical poetry disappears, he touches our contemporaries because he is already modern. His doctrine is nourished by tradition, but his psychology is closer to our own than to that of his sources. He certainly remains a mystery and his prestige appears ambiguous. He continues to irritate theologians. In the eyes of some, his behavior toward Abelard is a more vivid stain on his monk's tunic than his behavior toward the Canons of Lyon. But today, as in his own time, he enchants more readers than he exasperates. Why?

The answer can be formulated in a few words: St Bernard is a man of God. He is a man, and he knows the experiences of every man within himself; they are often feelings of intimate misery, and his should suffice to make us sympathetic toward his weaknesses and failings. He is a man of God: given to the Eternal One and possessed by him, Bernard received from him those lights and helps which are the same in all ages. He participated in the unfathomable mystery of Jesus Christ in his indefectible Church, always faithful to her divine origins, and yet, ever new because she receives her life from the God who is ever young. The message of this man is valid in our own days and for all manner of men: it is a universal message.

If he has his limitations, they are those imposed by his temperament and they appear less in his teaching than in his activity. He was occasionally the victim of his own gifts. If he had remained in the world, how seductive he would have been! He applied this facility to the service of God. There is a story that mothers feared for their daughters and husbands for their wives because he aroused their desire to follow his example and seek God in the cloister. It is true that he could only exercise this influence by leaving the cloister himself. The greatest minds understood this. St Hildegarde wrote to him: "You are mobile, but you are a support for others." After having reported Bernard's actions against Gilbert of Poitiers, which he himself had witnessed, John of Salisbury had the humility to write: "I cannot be convinced that such a holy man did not have zeal for the things of God." And, in this case, we can perhaps apply to Bernard the words which Newman wrote about St Cyril of Alexandria after having recalled, in "The Trials of Theodoret", the opposition that this bishop had suffered from Cyril at the Council of Ephesus:

> We could ask what should be our opinion of St Cyril.... Is he a saint? How can he be a saint, if all that has been reported above is historically true? I answer as follows: Cyril's faults are not

incompatible with great and heroic virtues—and
these he possessed. He had faith, constancy,
fearlessness, courage, endurance, perseverance;
and these virtues, along with contrition for his
failings, have wiped out his faults and preserved
him from due penalties. If martyrs obtain forgiveness of their sins by virtue of their martyrdom, it
is not so strange to say that there may exist other
sacrifices, other gestures of faith and charity,
which can be equally efficacious in earning the
divine mercy.

Finally, we must repeat, because this truth seems hard-
pressed to penetrate the minds in certain circles: Bernard
was not affected. He certainly possessed a great wealth of
sentiment, but this was not the determining factor in his
character or his work. If we had to find another adjective, we
could use the term "rhetorical". Bernard was animated by a
concern for literary beauty which led him to adopt the
expressions of his time and to place them at the service of his
work. One of the finest qualities of his heart was his tremendous energy; one of his intellectual gifts was that capacity for
assimilation which helped him to penetrate the ancient
doctrines, so much in harmony with his own thoughts, and
then translate them into his own fiery language. The mag-
nificence of his style and the power of his thought make him
a source in his own right. If he remains or becomes real once
again in our own days, unlike so many pseudo-Bernards from
the past, some of whom were indeed admirable, it is because
he is not sentimental like they were. Bernard's theology
remains solid, strongly based on St Paul, difficult and,
because of this, misunderstood by some; but his greatness
must be acknowledged.

A testimony from Maurice Blondel will finally serve to
situate him properly in the present as well as in the future:

Reading St Bernard and observing the New Testament, especially St Paul, have always made me
feel, from the beginning, that I am out of my

element in the intellectual world; and the more I wanted to be timely, the more I sought to surround myself, for such studies, with an atmosphere that is never dated, a philosophy that is like fresh air and is fully human, that can be just as breathable in the twenty-fifth century as it was in the second or the twelfth, and that only hopes to discover the here and now by first seeking the eternal which is ever relevant, even and especially when it seems inconsistent with the present.

FROM THE GIFTS OF GOD TO GOD HIMSELF

MANY COLLECTIONS OF EXCERPTS from St Bernard already exist. His work is so varied that it offers a vast selection and also the opportunity of dividing up the texts in different ways. In conformity with the aims of this small book, it seems fitting to illustrate here, in the light of testimonies borrowed from Bernard himself, the manner in which he conceived man's obligations with regard to his God-given gifts: talents, honors, even devotional graces should be used with detachment. When Bernard spoke of himself, it was for the general instruction of all; and what he said about and for others expressed what he had himself lived through.

We could have chosen numerous brief excerpts which would have been easier to read than the longer texts. However, it is the latter which truly reveal Bernard's "style" and his teaching method, as it was known and appreciated by his contemporaries. Important in each text is not only the sum of ideas expressed therein, but also the poetic atmosphere that Bernard has created, a kind of spiritual experience which he arouses by quoting the Bible and giving free rein to his imagination, fervor, and intelligence. Therefore, we have retained here only a small number of whole texts or sufficiently developed passages, preceded by an introduction which explains the nature of each. The patient effort required will not be without reward.

Bernard on Bernard

Introduction: Bernard, a little more than thirty years of age, an abbot for seven years, had just made Clairvaux' third foundation in 1121 at Foigny in the diocese of Laon.   He was already well-known, and Rainaud, who was one of his monks before being appointed abbot of Foigny, made a point of saying as much in a letter, associating himself with the praises of Bernard which resounded on all sides.   Bernard himself decided that this was the opportune moment to take a stand with regard to various tokens of esteem being lavished on him.   Around the years 1122-1123, he would write three letters to Rainaud and later unite them in a kind of dossier for inclusion in a collection of his letters when it came time to edit these.   Therefore, they are at once private correspondence and public documents.   In the first (72), he set the tone for his relationship with this superior of a house which continued to be dependent on Clairvaux and whose abbot was consequently still subject to him.   Bernard began by placing himself on an equal footing with Rainaud.   In the following letter (73), he counseled him to keep up his courage under the burden and to maintain an untiring benevolence toward those of his sons who proved to be difficult subjects. Rainaud must have previously complained, and Bernard replied with sympathetic concern.   Now the Abbot of Foigny did not respond, and, in a new letter (74), Bernard wrote that this silence hurt him: he is anxious about this man whom he loves.

In the first part of this record of friendship—which will be presented here—Bernard protested against the gratuitous honours which Rainaud had heaped upon him.   He did so in the opening salutation and justified his words again at the closing.   As was often his custom, he began by quoting the Bible: he bowed before the inspired words and took shelter in the authority of the Scriptures.   Then he went on to his own intimate experience, and this again was interpreted in the light of biblical texts.   Having introduced the theme of the "light burden", he developed it further by launching into the realm of imagination: symbols borrowed from the animal world were clarified by the Scriptures. Toward the end, he proclaimed his affection, revealed the meaning of the separation from which he suffered, and the last word was borrowed from the model of Christ. This piece of correspondence, where he displayed his talent for letter-writing, not without some degree of affectation but with a certain irony aimed at himself, is thus a charming lesson in humility and humanity.

Letter 72

TO his very dear Rainaud, from Bernard, not his father or his master, but his brother and comrade in service: all that one could wish for a very dear brother and comrade in service.

1. Do not be surprised, my dear Rainaud, if I dread all honorary titles: I feel unworthy of the reality which they conceal. For you to bestow these titles on me is a matter of social convention; acceptance of them would not be to my advantage. No doubt your concern is for the observance of these precepts: "Have a mutual respect for each other" (Rom. 12, 10); "Give way to one another in obedience to Christ" (Eph. 5, 20). But notice that they say: "mutual" and "one another". Therefore, they are intended for me as well as for you. You are also thinking of this phrase from the Rule: "Let the young honor their elders" (*Rule of St Benedict*, ch. 63). But to my mind come these maxims from another Rule, that which has Truth for its author: "The first will be last, the last will be first" (Matt 20, 16). "The greatest among you must behave as if he were the youngest" (Luke 22, 26). "They have made you master? Be among them as one of the rest." (Sir. 32, 1). "We are not dictators over your faith, but are fellow workers with you for your happiness" (II Cor 1, 24). "You, however, must not allow yourselves to be called Rabbi.... You must call no one on earth your father." (Matt 23, 8-9). Thus, as much as your compliments wish to raise me up, to that extent I feel crushed under the weight of these divine admonitions. I sing, or rather I weep, in the words of the psalm: "Having been

exalted, I was brought low and into despair" (Ps 88, 16).
"You have lifted me up and thrown me down" (Ps 102, 11).
But, with perhaps greater truth, I will say what I personally
feel: he who exalts me humbles me, and he who humbles me
exalts me. You believe that you are setting me on the
heights and you cast me to the ground; you wish to raise me
up and you oppress me.

Fortunately, these texts from the Truth and other similar
ones are there to console me. They put me down, but they
straighten me out; they cast me to the ground, but they teach
me a lesson; in such a way that my progress is measured by
my defeat and I can sing with complete joy: "It was good for
me to have to suffer, the better to learn your statutes. I put
the Law you have given before all the gold and silver in the
world." (Ps 119, 71-72).

2. How light is the burden of Truth! It is a joy as well as
a source of amazement. Light? But of course! Instead of
overwhelming the one who bears it, it is a comfort to him.
What could be lighter than a burden which is not an encum-
brance, which, on the contrary, supports the one who
supports it? Such a burden could well have swollen the
womb of a Virgin; He did not weigh her down. He allowed
himself to be carried in the arms of old Simeon, but he was in
fact the sustaining force. And it was he who ravished Paul
up to the third heaven, even when the Apostle was still
weighed down by corruptible flesh.

I look around me for an analogy and I consider the feathers
of the birds. In a unique manner, they enlarge the body
which they cover and yet, at the same time, they make it
more agile. A marvel of nature! The very thing that
increases the matter also relieves the burden; as the mass
increases, so the gravity decreases. We can see how
enlightening this comparison is: like the burden of Christ,
the feathers bear those who bear them.

Shall I speak of the quadriga? You harness beasts of
burden to it and the burden which they could not haul is
definitely augmented but, at the same time, becomes trans-
portable. Weight is added on to weight, and the whole

becomes less heavy. Likewise, consider the painful burden of the law. We bring on the quadriga of the Gospel: perfection grows and the difficulty diminishes. As it is said: "Swiftly runs his word" (Ps 147, 15). A word which was once known only in Judea and whose own weight prevented it from traveling farther—did it not make the hands of Moses himself fall from weariness? (Ex. 17, 11-12). Grace makes it light; it is placed on evangelical wheels and thereby diffuses itself throughout the land, flying with great speek to the very ends of the earth.

But I see that I am getting verbose!

3. So, my dear friend, please do not weigh me down with honors that are not rightfully mine. Otherwise, despite your good intentions, you will have a place among those who bear a grudge against me. I am speaking of those men about whom I often complain to God—and only to God—in these terms: "Those who used to praise me now use me as a curse" (Ps 102, 9). And God replies to my pleading; he knows it is well-founded: "Those who pronounce you blessed lead you astray" (Is 3, 12). And I cry out: "Let them quickly retreat, covered with shame, those who say to me: Very good! Very good!" (Ps. 70, 4).

However, I would not want this to be interpreted as an imprecation or malediction directed toward any particular adversaries. All I ask of God is that he drive away those who think of me as superior to what they actually see in me or hear about me. Let them be kept away, that is, let them renounce those exaggerations due to ignorance and retract their fine speeches. How can they do this? By acquiring a better knowledge of the one whom they praised, and consequently, by being ashamed both of their error and of the little that can actually be made of their friend. It is in this way that I would like to see far from me and covered with confusion not only those who truly wish me ill and merely praise me from self-interest, but those who do me harm inadvertently, admiring me with good intentions but to excess. I would like to appear so vile and hateful in their eyes that they would be ashamed of having sung the praises of such an individual and would take care not to do so again. Against the former I say: "Oh, let them turn back in confusion who delight in my harm!" (Ps 70, 3). And against the latter: "Let them quickly retreat, covered with shame, those who say to me: Very good! Very good!" (Ps 70, 4).

4. To get back to you; as you can see, I have rejected with reason the great titles of master and father with which you desired to honor and not burden me; and, to this end, I have armed myself with the shield of truth. I have reminded you that, according to the Apostle's example, I must not seek to dominate your virtue, but simply rejoice along with you; and I have quoted the words of the Lord which say that we have but one Father, who is in heaven, and we are all brothers. I have also wanted to call myself your brother and your comrade in service: we share in the same heritage, we are in the same state. If I wished to usurp that which belongs to God alone, I would be fearful of hearing his reproach: "If I am Lord, where is the fear that is due me? If I am Father, where is the honor that is mine?" (Mal 1, 6).

Of course, I do not deny that I have for you a father's affection. I merely object to the authority which is implied in this title. Yes, the affection that I feel for you is not less than what a father feels for his son.

5. Now, to return to the rest of your letter: I could mourn over your absence as you do over mine—you hardly conceal the fact—if I did not have to prefer the will of God over our own affectionate sentiments and personal benefit. Otherwise—I mean, if Christ were not an issue—how could I ever bear to have you so far from me, you who are my dearest companion, the most necessary, the most obedient in the execution of my requests, the most active in research, the most useful when it comes to discussing a problem, the quickest to refresh my memory? Blessed are we if we persevere in this way to the end, never having our own interest in view, but only that of Jesus Christ!

BERNARD THE BIBLICAL PREACHER

Moral Reflection on Naaman and the Seven Baths

Introduction: The Abbot of Clairvaux composed some great literary sermons for the purpose of publication. But he also spoke familiarly to his monks and, when the occasion presented itself, to other audiences. Some of those who had listened to him later wrote down these conferences and the following is an example. Several different versions are in existence, but their basic harmony on the essentials is enough to guarantee that they do indeed convey the teaching of St Bernard and his simple language, that "oral style" in which he excelled as surely as in his polished prose.

Here he is commenting on that passage from the Fourth Book of Kings which provided the first reading in the Mass on Monday of the third week in Lent. "Mellifluous" in the traditional sense of the term—which he recalls at the beginning—he will draw from that beeswax, the literal meaning, the honey which constitutes the moral sense. His interpretation is not as arbitrary as it might seem at first: we will see it include a constant reference to the sacred text. Furthermore, for the explanation of proper names—and there are a number of them—he refers back to etymologies received from the Old Testament and rabbinical tradition, transmitted to the Middle Ages by St Jerome.

From the start, the problem concerns the gifts of God: should one glory in what has been received? Bernard makes use of the Socratic precept "Know thyself", in which Gilson has perceived one of the clues to an understanding of his entire teaching. Then the themes of conversion and humility are lovingly developed. At the center of everything is the mystery of Christ. Every aspect of his work is present: the prophets and St John the Baptist, the Apostles and the martyrs, the angels and the whole Church are there as witnesses. At the end, the moral of the seven baths is disclosed. Bernard must have given this talk with a smile reminiscent of St Gregory the Great and of St Francis de Sales. He enchanted his listeners, while constantly turning their thoughts toward Christ.

Sermon

"NAAMAN, captain of the army of the King of Syria, was a great and wealthy man, but also a leper. And he had in his house, as a servant, a young girl from the land of Israel" (IV Kings 5, 1-2).

That is the basic plot of the story that we are considering. History is the threshing-floor of doctrine, where good narrators separate the grain from the straw with the flail of diligence and the winnowing machine of research. Just as honey is hidden under the beeswax and the nut inside the shell, so beneath the surface of the story lies the sweetness of the moral.

"Naaman" can be translated as "beauty" or "beautiful" and signifies the wealthy of this world who appear powerful and illustrious in their own eyes. Such men, endowed with abundant riches, boastful of family titles, proud of the high quality of their relationships, having some knowledge of literature and of law, are nevertheless leprous by virtue of their various crimes. Enriched by the production of wheat, wine and oil, they are a cause and occasion of sin. They are fairly inclined to vice, well-prepared for crime, sufficiently exempt for injustice, according to what is written: "Their iniquity oozes like fat" (Ps 72, 7). However, when their time comes for mercy (Ps 101, 14) and their time to be visited (Jer 46, 21), they receive the counsels of a young girl.

"Following the counsel of the young girl, he went to

Eliseus and knocked on the door of his house." Eliseus means "salvation of the Lord". It is Jesus, the Lord of the world, who saved his people from their sins (Matt 1, 21), and of whom the prophet says: "Your salvation, God has received me" (Ps 68, 30). And he says of himself: "I am the salvation of the people" (Ps 34, 3). His dwelling place is Sacred Scripture, or the Church, or many religious persons in whom he lives by his grace. The door is repentance, by which we enter him and he enters us. As it is written: "When you speak again, I will say: Here I am" (*cf* Is 58, 9). And these words: "Come back to me and I will come back to you" (Mal 3, 7). We have turned away from him and he has turned away from us. Let us return to him and he will return to us.

Eliseus remained sitting in the house and sent his servant with these words: "Go down to the Jordan and wash yourself seven times and you will be purified." (*Cf* IV Kings 5, 10). Our Eliseus has been lifted up bodily, he is seated at the right hand of the Father, that is in those higher places which are not yet visible to us. But he has sent his servant. This servant is the intellect or pure reason, made in the image of God (Gen 1, 27). It is this servant who was the sole survivor of the massacre of daughters and sons and reported the fact to Job (Job 1, 18-19). Or else this servant is the Holy Spirit who makes us children: that is, naive in the way of malice, and childlike in our simplicity. Or again, the servant is Sacred Scripture by reason of the purity of its discourses and its chaste words (Ps 11, 7).

Therefore, this servant says: Come down from Syria, that is "the high place"—Syria, in fact, means "sublime"—and go to the Jordan, that is toward the likeness of Christ which is humility. For the devil's title is pride and Christ's title is humility. In fact, he proposed himself as Master of the school of this discipline, saying: "I do not send you to the oracles of the prophets or to enigmas; in my school, you will learn that I am meek and humble of heart. (Matt 11, 29). I offer myself to you as a mirror." But exterior humility has little value without the inner reality, that is true obedience.

Here are the three things required of you: that your heart be
the seat of humility, that your words reflect your patience,
that you persevere in your works. The words themselves
agree in this way: Go down to the Jordan. "Jordan" in fact
means "descent", and it is one of the reasons why the Lord
especially chose this river for his own Baptism. (Matt 3, 13).
"Wash yourself seven times", that is "perfectly".
"Naaman replied indignantly: 'Are not the rivers of
Damascus, the Abana and the Farfar, worth more than all the
waters of Israel? I could have bathed there and been
purified'." (IV Kings 5, 11-12). Damascus means "drinking
blood"; it is the people who are drunk with delight over our
eternal death by the bloody beverage of sin. "Farfar" means
"mole", that blind and ugly little animal who makes his
home in the bowels of the earth and in holes, undermining
gardens and plants. It signifies the avid desire for earthly
goods, those men who have decided to keep their eyes fixed
on the ground (Ps 16, 11). It is that crippled woman whom
the Lord healed (Luke 13, 11-13). "Abana" in Latin means
"his stones"; this designates certain great men in the Church
or in the world. Churchmen, according to these words: "The
stones of the sanctuary were strewn in the corners of every
square" (Lam 4, 1); worldly men, according to words from
this same prophet: "Babylon gathers stones along the way"
(Unidentified). Those who abandon the beauty of humility
are ambitious for honors. This is what they answer every day
when we tell them not to place their trust in visible things:
"Is it not better to possess riches, to be of good cheer (*cf*
Luke 13, 11-13), to have a soft bed, to go one's own way and
delight in honors, rather than waste away under daily
afflictions?" This is what is meant by: "Are they not worth
more than all the waters of Israel,the Abana and the Farfar?"
(IV Kings 5, 13).

His military aides and his acolytes said to him: Even if the
prophet had prescribed something very difficult, you would
surely have done it; how much more so when he merely tells
you: "Wash yourself and you will be clean." These acolytes
are the guardian angels and religious men who say: "Even if

what is prescribed was beyond your strength, you would have had to carry it out." And they offer, by way of example, Peter's cross, Paul's sword, Vincent's sawing-trestle, Lawrence's gridiron; and even our camel had to pass through the eye of a needle (Matt 19, 24), that is, Christ went through the agony of the Passion (St Gregory, *Moralia* 1, 21). If we consider all of this, even if something difficult is commanded, we must not refuse because "the sufferings" of this life can never be compared with the glory that is to come." (Rom 8, 18).

Even if it is something difficult.... In the first creation, God gave me to myself; in the regeneration, he restored me to myself, he gave himself up for me. What tremendous thing can I do for such a gift, for such a great price that has been paid for me? "How can I repay the Lord for all that he has given me?" (Ps 115, 12). "I will die", says the prophet; for that is the meaning of: "I will take up the chalice of salvation." (Ps 115, 13).

"Following their advice, he went down and bathed seven times in the Jordan" (IV Kings 5, 14). There are seven baths or purifications: the bath outside of the body, the bath around the body, the bath on the body, two for the tongue and two for the spirit.

The bath outside of the body is the renunciation of all riches and possessions which are called "exterior" because they do not touch the body and are not part of its substance.

The second bath, around the body, is contempt for expensive garments. For, if it were not a sin to wear an expensive garment, the Apostle would not say: "No expensive garments" (I Tim 2, 9). Moreover, if it was not praiseworthy to wear a poor garment, we would not have such abundant testimony, such marked approval from Christ on the subject of John and Elias who wore poor clothing (*cf* IV Kings 1, 8; Matt 3, 4; Mark 1, 6). Jacob also says: "If the Lord my God has given me bread, it is to eat; and a garment is to clothe myself." (Gen 28, 20). He did not say that it was to glory in, but to cover his nakedness.

The third bath, on the body, is the mortification of the

members, the chastisement of the body. According to these words of Paul: "I chastise my body and force it to serve me." (I Cor 9, 27). This flesh is Agar in conflict with her mistress (Gen 16), of which Ambrose says: "It is inevitable that she who was robed in insolence should utter abuse." Our flesh is a wanton animal, a brazen donkey, but we must chastise it so that it will obey its mistress.

There are two baths for the tongue: to avoid boastful speech in times of success, if perchance God should grant prosperity in earthly or spiritual goods, and to guard against an impatient word in times of adversity. He who is justly punished and demonstrates his impatience is companion to the thief who hung on the left side of Christ (Luke 23, 39). He who is justly punished and remains patient is like the thief on the right who said: "We are paying a just price for our actions." (Luke 23, 41).

There are two baths for the spirit: renouncing one's own will and not presuming to defend one's own personal opinions. Self-will must be renounced so that he who maintains an exterior silence, in both prosperity and adversity, does not retain his own willful notions within, for fear that he might become like the devil. Just as God wished to be the one source of all things, so anyone who retains his own will without submitting it to God has set up his own whims as another source. One should not overestimate one's own wisdom; some even appeal to the authority of Scripture to silence others and support their own opinions.

These seven baths existed in Christ. The exterior bath because, rich as he was, he made himself poor for our sakes. The bath around the body, because, at his birth, he was wrapped in swaddling clothes and placed in a manger (Luke 2, 7). On the body, because he fasted (Matt 4, 2) and spent nights in prayer (Luke 6, 12). For the tongue: he did not falter in times of success because, when they wanted to make him king, he fled (Jn 6, 15). He did not weaken in the face of adversity because, like a sheep before the shearer, he remained silent (Is 53, 7). His heart was bathed becase he did not come to do his own will, but that of his Father (Jn 6,

38), and he preferred divine counsels to those of Peter who said: "This will never happen to you, Lord" (Matt 16, 22). Furthermore, when Joseph and his mother said to him: "Son, why have you done this to us?" he replied: "I must be about my Father's business." And still he followed them and was subject to them (Luke 2, 48, 51).

"And his flesh became like the flesh of a child" (IV Kings 5, 14), that is, in the likeness of Christ. It is this child of whom it is written: "A child is born to us" (Is 9, 6). Adam lost his dignity, his innocence, his immortality. These three things were restored to us by this Child. It is the seventh bath of Naaman in the Jordan.

BERNARD THE REFORMER

Introduction: Although he spoke in a familiar way to his monks, Bernard knew how to create an air of solemnity when he addressed important men. Here is how he reminded the prelates of their duties by addressing himself to one of their number: Henri de Boisrogues, one of the highest dignitaries of the Church in France, who was known as "Aper" or the "wild boar". Having become Archbishop of Sens in 1122, he had been attacked—Bernard went so far as to say he was "persecuted"—by the King of France, Louis the Fat. The Abbot of Clairvaux had taken on his defense at the time in three letters (epp. 49, 50, 51) sent to Pope Honorius II and his chancellor Cardinal Aymeric. Nevertheless, the Archbishop of Sens was finally deposed in 1136; he died in 1142. He seems to have been an obstinate and authoritarian character. Having defended him, Bernard had some right to his good will. He later wrote to him on behalf of the monks of Molesmes (epp. 43, 44) and others (ep. 316); he reproached him sharply with regard to certain errors in his manner of governing (ep. 182). He who was only an abbot could speak to this archbishop with authority and even with a degree of pungency—*"mordacius"*, he himself called it.

For his part, this prelate seems to have manifested enough humility to seek Bernard's counsel. The saint took advantage of this request to draw up a treatise in the form of a letter, addressed to the recipient and to all of the clergy: *On the Duties and Conduct of Bishops.* Soon after presenting the matter in question, he demonstrates his strong opposition to the ostentation of Churchmen; in this respect, he preaches love of the poor and poverty, and other virtues of the priest (ep. 42, n. 4-12).

Letter 42, On the Duties of Bishops, II, 4-7

YOU will honor your ministry (*cf* Rom 11, 13) not by wearing fine garments, nor by the splendor of your entourage, nor by the size of your buildings, but by honorable conduct, concern for things of the spiritual order, and the practice of good works.

How many act otherwise! It is evident that among certain bishops there is great anxiety over their wardrobes, but little or no zeal for virtue. I would like to remind them of the Apostle's words: "No sumptuous garments!" (I Tim 2, 9), but I fear that they might be offended to have applied to them an admonition addressed to the lowlier sex, to persons of an inferior order. As if doctors did not use the same lancet to operate on kings and criminals! As if we would insult the head by using the same scissors to cut the hair as were used to trim the nails! If our good bishops consider that it is beneath their dignity to be implicated with silly females in one and the same condemnation—pronounced by the Apostle, not by me—let them avoid falling into similar errors! Let them refuse to glory in the work of weavers and furriers rather than in their own! Let them be ashamed to cover their consecrated hands which serve for consecration with those fine red-tinted skins called "gules". Nor let them use any to cover their breasts: it would be better to decorate themselves with the precious stone of wisdom. Nor around their necks: the yoke of Christ would lie more decently and with greater sweetness!

Such ornaments cannot compare with the stigmata of Christ; and it is this which bishops should display on their bodies, following the example of the martyrs. Let us leave baubles for the women. They have only worldly things on their minds and are anxious to please their husbands: whence stems their usual concern regarding dress.

But you, a priest of the Most High God: whom do you wish to please? If it is the world, what good is it for you to be a priest? If it is God, then why "like people, like priest"? You cannot serve two masters. "He who wishes to be the friend of the world becomes the enemy of God" (James 4, 4). And the prophet writes: "God scatters the bones of those who would be pleasing to me; they are disgraced because God has rejected them" (Ps 52, 6). And the Apostle: "If I sought to please men, I would not be the servant of Christ" (Gal 1, 10). If you wish to please men, you will not please God; if you do not please God, neither will you appease him. As I have said: what then is the good of being a priest? And if it is not the world that you wish to please, but God, then why: "like people, like priest"? The bishop is the shepherd, the people are his flock: is it fitting that the shepherd should appear no way different from his sheep? Will my shepherd go along like me, a poor sheep, walking with his head bent toward the soil, always looking at the earth, empty-headed, thinking only of his stomach?... Woe to me when the wolf comes! No one will be there to run up, having foreseen the blow, and snatch me from his teeth. Is it fitting for the shepherd to live only by his senses, to become attached to the most vile things, to yearn for the goods of this earth? Should he not rather stand up like a man, look up to heaven, seek and taste the things that are above?...

But there is my man, indignant at the least sign from me; there he is ordering me to keep my mouth shut, reminding me that a simple monk has no right to pass judgment on bishops. That's fine with me! Only have me shut my eyes also, that I may not see that which you forbid me to criticize.

Such great presumption for the sake of truth! I can see two cruel she-wolves, vanity and a taste for luxury, hurling themselves at the shepherd. I tremble with fear and I bleat, believing that someone will run to the rescue of this man in danger. What will they do to a poor little sheep like me if they can attack the shepherd himself with such ferocity? And if he does not want me to cry out for his sake, will he not allow me to do so for my own? Let it be! However, let us keep silence for fear that my mouth will appear to be storming the heavens (*cf* Ps 72, 9); the Church will continue to exclaim: "No sumptuous garments!" (I Tim 2, 9). The words are directed at women; but so that the bishop may be ashamed to discover in himself what is objected to in the weaker sex.

Will it put an end to his humiliation if I cease to mutter through my teeth? Will each one's conscience also remain silent? And what would happen if, quite by chance, someone ventured to cite these words which are not from the Gospel, nor a prophet, nor even an ecclesiastical author, but a pagan: "Tell me, you who are pontiffs, what is that gold doing (he does not say: in the sanctuary; there it would be tolerated, but) on your horses' bit?" (Persius, *Satires*, II, 69).

I would like to be still: the misery of the poor will cry out. Public opinion will keep silence, hunger will not. Ah, yes! Public opinion will keep still, for "the world cannot hate you" (Jn 7,7). How can the world condemn sin when, on the contrary, it "praises the desires of the sinner and speaks well of rogues"? (Ps 10, 3).

Those who cry out are the ill-clad, the starving. Listen to their moaning: "Tell us, you who are pontiffs, what is that gold doing on your horses' bit?" Would it be there to drive away hunger and cold? For us who suffer these things, what good are those overcoats, either suspended from hangers or folded among your baggage? We are the ones who suffer from your prodigality; it is from us that you mercilessly take away what you spend!

And yet, like you, we are God's creatures, we have been redeemed by the Blood of Christ. Thus we are your brothers. See now: your brothers' portion serves the pleasure of your eyes, our lives have less worth than your superfluous goods, your vanity grows to the extent that our basic needs are stripped away.

Two evils thus spring up from a single root: covetousness leads you astray by involving you in frivolity; it kills us by

stripping us bare. Your horses prance by, covered with
precious stones; and you pay no heed to our bare feet. We
can see the heads of your mules decorated with rings, chains,
bells, harnesses marked with golden nails, all kinds of things,
as beautiful as they are costly; and you do not even have a bit
of cloth for your brothers in need.

Besides all this, you have not acquired all of this wealth by
trade, nor by the work of your hands, nor by right of
inheritance, unless you say in your hearts: "Make us
masters, as by inheritance, of the sanctuary of God" (Ps 89,
13).

The complaints which I have attributed here to the poor are
only uttered in the presence of God, before the One to whom
their hearts speak. Never would they dare to oppose you
openly, knowing that they have a greater need to make their
supplications heard. But the day will come when they will
stand with perfect confidence in the face of those who have
reduced them to misery. At that moment, their defender will
be the Father of orphans, the Judge who accedes to the
widow's complaints. Then we will hear these words: "In so
far as you did not do this for one of these little ones who
belong to Me, you neglected to do it for Me." (Matt 25, 40).

BERNARD ON UNION WITH CHRIST

Introduction: Bernard was especially fond of the Feast of the Ascension, because the mystery which is celebrated is the culmination of all those which came before: it is the return of the Incarnate Word to the Father after he has, by his examples and teachings and then by his suffering and Resurrection, accomplished the work which had been given him, and whose fruit will be the Holy Spirit, sent by the Father and himself. For christians, the Lord's departure is a call to detachment: their minds must not cease to contemplate his actions. But faith must purify their intelligence, their need for affectivity, so that, without delighting in the sensible presence of the Lord, they may prove their love by consenting to the demands of his will. Here again, the prophets of the Old Covenant are referred to as prototypes of the mystery realized in the Ascension, models of the attitude which should be adopted by the disciples of Christ. Borrowing from Origen, Bernard quoted and interpreted, in this respect, a verse from *Lamentations* concerning the shadows in which we live and the obscure light which is already a source of joy. The Virgin Mary is mentioned in relation to her Son. Finally, all will be consummated in the glory of Christ's return on the last day.

Like other Cistercians, Bernard was opposed to anything that could appear ostentatious in the liturgy of the monks. But on the day of the Ascension, he introduced at Clairvaux a procession which was soon adopted in all of the abbeys of the

Order. In an intimate sermon addressed to his community, the memory of which has been preserved for us by his secretary, Geoffrey of Auxerre, he drew great pleasure in imagining at length the solemn entry of Christ into his kingdom, to the chanting of angels' choirs acclaiming him as he passed. In the text, which he prepared for publication and which we will now read, he was more sober in detail, but he did give a fine interpretation of the meaning of the mystery recalled by this procession ritual. It represents the return of Christ, as well as our own return, to the Father in the Holy Spirit.

Sermon II for the Ascension

1. **M**Y very dear brothers: this is a glorious and joyous solemnity by which a unique glory is conferred on Christ and a joy that is no less rare is given to us. Today indeed marks the culmination and the ultimate end of the other liturgical feasts, the blessed final step in the journey undertaken by the Son of God. "The one who descended is also the one who has ascended" today "above all the heavens to fill all things" (Eph 4, 10). He had proven that he was the master of all things, on earth, in the sea, and in the lower regions. It only remained for him to demonstrate by similar, though stronger argument, that he was Lord of the air and the heavens.

The earth recognized its master when, at the sound of the powerful voice which cried: "Lazarus, come out!" (Jn 11, 42), it obeyed by restoring the dead man confined within it. The sea had known him and become solid under his feet (and the apostles had believed they were seeing a ghost!). The lower regions had known him because he had broken down the bronze gates and the iron bars that had held them closed, and he had bound up that insatiable murderer who is called the devil and Satan.

Indeed, he who has raised the dead, purified the lepers, opened the eyes of the blind, healed the lame, chased away sickness with a breath, has shown himself to be master of all things: with the same hand that created them, he recreated those which had broken down.

At another time, he predicted that a coin would be found in the mouth of a fish about to be hauled in; it is evident from this that the sea and all that moved within it was subject to him.

Finally, he who indicted the angelic powers and nailed them to his cross (*cf* Col 2, 14-15) has obviously received authority over the official quarters of the lower regions. Indeed he is the one who "went about doing good and curing all who had fallen into the power of the devil" (Acts 10, 38), who stood up on a rocky plateau to preach to the multitudes (*cf* Luke 6, 17), who stood before the govenor to receive his blows: always standing, tiring himself out in every way and working out our salvation on earth (Ps 74, 12) all the time that he was seen here below and lived among men. (Bar 3, 38).

2. Lord Jesus, in order to close your seamless garment, to perfect the integrity of our faith, all that remains is for you to reveal yourself to your disciples as master of the air by rising high above the heavens. At which point, it will be well proven that you are the master of all, for you will have filled all things. Then, at your name, every knee will bend, in heaven, on earth, and under the earth, and every tongue will proclaim that you are in the glory of the Father (*cf* Phil 2, 10-11) and at his right hand. This is indeed where we rejoice in eternal delights, and this is why the Apostle urges us to seek the things that are above, those to be found where Christ is seated at the right hand of God (Col 3, 1); for, there too, certainly, our treasure is Jesus Christ, "he in whom are hidden all the treasures of wisdom and of knowledge" (Col 2, 3), he "in whose body dwells the fullness of divinity" (Col 2, 9).

3. What do you think, my brothers? What grief and what fear must have seized the hearts of the apostles when they saw their Lord taken up from them, when they saw him carried up through the air, not on the rungs of a ladder, nor pulled by ropes—though he was escorted by angels, he was not supported by them—but rising by the sheer super-abundance of his own power! (*cf* Is 63, 1). Then was accom-

plished what he had foretold: There where I am, you cannot come" (Jn 13, 33). Wherever he would have gone on this earth, they would have followed without ever separating themselves from him. They had even walked on the sea in pursuit of him, at the risk of sinking—as Peter had done at one time. But where he is not going, they cannot follow, for, "a corruptible body weighs down the soul and this earthly dwelling place burdens the mind with a thousand thoughts" (Wisdom 9, 15). Also, their grief is very great: they see him for whom they have left all things now withdrawn from their sight and their touch. How could the sons of the Spouse refrain from weeping at the moment when the Spouse is taken from them? And how great their fear when they saw themselves left as orphans, abandoned in the midst of the Jews! For they had not yet been robed in the strength that comes from on high (*cf* Luke 24, 49).

Thus, blessing them, he was taken up into heaven; and undoubtedly his feelings of incomparable mercy were moved by the distress of his poor little novices: if it had not been part of his task to prepare a place for them, if he had not known that it was best for them that he remove his corporal presence.

What joy, what a fitting procession! The holy souls, the heavenly powers lead him in triumph to the Father, and there he sits at his right hand! Truly it is on this day that he fills all things: born among men, having lived with them, having suffered even unto death at the hands of men and for their sakes, he is now there risen, exalted, and forever seated at the right hand of God. I recognize the tunic woven all in one piece from top to bottom (Jn 19, 23). This enthronement has closed it off. The Lord Jesus Christ has, from this moment, attained his fullness and he has himself filled all things.

4. But actually, how do these feasts affect me? Who will console me, Lord Jesus? I did not see you hanging from the cross, your livid body marked by blows. I did not bear the sufferings with the Crucified One, nor pay my final respects to the dead. I would have at least alleviated your wounds by my tears. How could you depart, without so much as taking

leave of me, on the day when, as the true King of Glory, robed in splendor, you ascended to the highest heavens?

I believe my soul would have refused to be consoled if the angels had not advised me, saying in joyous tones: "Men of Galilee, why do you stand looking up to heaven? This Jesus who has been taken on high, far away from you, will come again in the same way as you have seen him going up to heaven" (Acts 1, 11). They say: "He will come in the same way." Are they speaking of that unique and yet universal procession in which, preceded by the angels and followed by all men, he will come to judge the living and the dead? Yes, he will come in the same way; but it will be as he ascended, not as he descended. He was humble when he came to save souls; he will be sublime when he comes to raise this corpse and make it like unto a glorious body. The more fragile the receptacle, the greater will be the honors bestowed on it. At that moment, he will be seen in all his power and majesty, he who had once hidden himself beneath the weakness of the flesh. These words apply to me also: "I will contemplate him, but not at this time; I will see him, but not just now" (Numbers 24, 17); and this second glorification will offer evidence that will surpass the first.

5. In the meantime, he has been taken up to the right hand of the Father and he stands before his face on our behalf. He is seated at his right hand, with mercy at his own right, and judgment at his left. His mercy is abundant and so is his judgment. On the right, water; on the left, fire: and he holds both with a firm hand. "His mercy has been confirmed for those who fear him; it is greater than the distance between earth and heaven" (Ps 103, 11). God's designs on them are immutable: "his mercy for those who fear him is for all eternity and forever" (Ps 103, 17): for all eternity by predestination, forever by glorification.

The same holds for reprobates: "He appears terrible before the sons of men" (Ps 66, 5). On one side as on the other, the sentence does not change; it fixes for eternity those who are saved as well as those who perish. Who knows which of you here before my eyes have their names written in the heavens and recorded in the book of predestination? Yet, I seem to notice signs of your calling, your justification, in the humble lives that you lead. You can well imagine how my bones would thrill with joy if I were completely sure of this! But "man does not know whether he is worthy of love or hatred" (Wisdom 9, 1).

6.   My beloved, you must persevere in the lessons which you have learned: raise yourselves up by humility. That is the way: there is no other. He who seeks to make progress some other way falls more quickly than he climbs. Humility alone exalts and leads to life. As God, Christ could not grow, since there is nothing greater than God. He did find a means of growth by coming down, however, taking on our flesh, suffering and dying to save us from eternal death. Then God exalted him, Jesus rose from the dead, ascended, and is seated at the right hand of God. "Go and do likewise" (Luke 10, 37). It is impossible for you to ascend unless you begin by descending. That is an eternal law: "He who exalts himself will be humbled; he who humbles himself will be exalted" (Luke 14, 11).

Oh, what bewilderment! The folly of the sons of Adam! Ascending is a very difficult thing; there is nothing easier than descending. But no! They ascend without constraint, whereas they are at great pains to accept descent. One can see that they are always ready to accept honors and ecclesiastical dignities: honors and dignities which the angels themselves would fear to take on their shoulders. But when it comes to following you, Lord Jesus, one can find hardly any who are willing to let themselves be carried away, or who will allow themselves to be led along the way of your commandments.

It is noteworthy, however, that some are carried away; and those can say: "Draw us after you" (Song of Songs 1, 3). Others are led, and they say: "The King has brought me to his chamber" (Song of Songs 1, 3). Finally, there are others who are ravished, like the Apostle who was caught up to the third heaven (cf II Cor 12, 2). The first are blessed: in their patience they possess their souls (Luke 21, 19). The second, who confess voluntarily, are more blessed. But the most blessed of all are the third: their free will is, so to speak, buried in the depths of God's mercy; the fervor of the spirit ravishes them to the heights of glory. In the body? Out of the body? They do not know. All they know is that they are ravished.

Blessed is he, Lord Jesus, for whom you are ever the guide! Such a one is not like that soul, that fugitive, who wished to ascend without delay and was struck by the right hand of the divinity. May we "your people, the sheep of your pastures" (Ps 79, 13), follow you, travel through you and to you, for you are the way, the truth, and the life: the way, by your example; the truth, by your promise; the life, as our reward. "You have the words of eternal life; we know and we believe that you are the Christ, the Son of God" (Jn 6, 69-70), "God Himself, Most High over all things, blessed forever" (Rom 9, 5).

BERNARD ON GOD

Introduction: In the treatise *On Consideration* which was dedicated to Pope Eugene III, Bernard followed in his own original way a plan inspired by a page from St Augustine which has influenced a whole series of authors, including Goethe. He speaks successively to the recipient—and through him to all men—of that which is in him, beneath him, around him, and above him. It is this last point which he covers in Book V. He recalls the heavenly Jerusalem and its inhabitants. With regard to the blessed spirits, he discusses the functions proper to each of the nine angelic choirs and their relation to God. Then he comes to the haunting question which will furnish the theme for the latter part of the treatise: "What is God?" It is as if Bernard were rising higher and higher into the mystery of God Himself: his nature, his unity, the Trinity of persons, the union of humanity with the Word in the Incarnation. And for the eighth time, in the passage which will be quoted here, he repeats the leitmotif: "What then is God?"

The theme which he develops at this peak point is that of the four dimensions of charity proposed by St Paul. As St Augustine had done, Bernard associated these with the idea of the different objects of charity, which all lead to God. Is the image of the quadriga a recollection from Plato's *Phaedra*? Some have thought so. More probably the abbot of Clairvaux was reminded here of Paschasius Radbertus or some medieval author who had explained the same allegory.

But Bernard used it in his own inimitable way. He did not apply it only to the four cardinal virtues as others had done, but abandoned himself to subtle variations on man's attitudes in the presence of God. As befits this type of compendium, a summary of all that concerns the transcendance of the mystery of God, the tone is sublime: it is as if he wished to have the reader judge God from the point of view of God himself as we will see him in eternity. *Comprehendere*: this word taken from St Paul does not mean "to know" or "to understand", but "to seize" or "apprehend". It is evident that the vocabulary remains biblical and moral lessons are not overlooked: this exalted teaching is still within the reach of man. Nevertheless, his application of these lessons in his practical life is founded on doctrine, and this, as Bernard always insisted, results from a union of faith and intellect.

On Consideration, Book Five, XIII, 27-31

WHAT is God? He is length, breadth, height, depth. "Now what!" you say. "We hear you preaching a quaternity, which you recently held in abhorrence." Not at all: I have held it in abhorrence and I always will. I have spoken of several things in appearance only: it is really one alone. I simply wanted to define, according to our ability to grasp and not according to his condition, the God who is One. Such divisions correspond to our own minds, not to God Himself. Our manner of speaking about him is diverse, our ways of going toward him are many but they all have only one meaning and they all apply to only one God.

No, these four words which I have used do not express divisions of the divine substance, nor dimensions such as we see in physical bodies, nor distinct persons like the cnes we adore in the Trinity. It is hardly a question of enumerating properties such as those that we recognize in these Persons, even though they are not different from these persons. Their meaning is completely other. Each one of the four terms of this definition of God represents nothing less than the whole; and the whole in turn represents nothing more than each taken by itself.

The fact is that we are totally incapable of aspiring to the simplicity of God! Do we claim to conceive him as One? He presents himself to our minds as quadruple. What produces this illusion is the fact that, for the moment, we are not permitted to see God other than by symbols and reflections.

But, when we see him face to face, we will see him as he is. On that day, we will be able to lean as heavily as we wish on our fragile bit of intelligence; it will neither disappear nor be broken to pieces. It will only acquire greater firmness and cohesion; it will adjust itself to the unity of God, or better yet, to the Unity *par excellence*, by which one single image will respond to the image of Unity. Yes, by seeing God as he is, we will become like unto him (I Jn 3, 2). What a blessed prospect! It is with this thought in mind that the psalmist cried out with justifiable longing: "My glance has sought you, Lord; I will not cease to desire your countenance!" (Ps 26, 8).

Since our task is to seek until we receive further orders, let us climb onto this quadriga, which is the best we have at the moment. This vehicle is necessary for us who are weak and sickly. Let us see if even we can seize the meaning of which has seized us: that is, the *raison d'etre* of this chariot which carries us along.

It is in fact our conductor, he who was the first to point out its use, who offers us this counsel. According to him, we must apply ourselves "to seize, with all the saints, the length and the breadth, the height and the depth" (Eph 3, 18).

St Paul said "seize" and not "know". We must not limit our search to the areas of reason; we must desire its fruit with all our powers. The fruit does not lie in knowledge, but in the act of seizing. As another Apostle says elsewhere: "It is a sin to know what is right and not do it." (James 4, 17). And it is St Paul again in another one of his writings who offers this counsel: "Act like the runners in the stadium. Run to seize the prize of the course." (I Cor 9, 24). But what is meant by this word "to seize"? I will explain it to you in a moment.

What then is God? I have said that God is length. What do we mean by length? Eternity, whose length is such that it knows no limits, neither in time nor in space.

God is also breadth. What do we mean by breadth? Charity. But here again how can we encompass the charity of God within limits, this God "who hates nothing that he has created"? (Wisdom 11, 25). For it is he "who makes the sun rise on the good and the wicked, who makes the rain fall on the just and the unjust." (Matt 5, 45). Thus God opens his heart even to his enemies. But, not content with this, he extends his charity to infinity. And this charity surpasses not only all that the heart can feel, but all that the mind can conceive. This is what the Apostle is saying when he adds: "We must realize that the love of Jesus Christ is beyond all knowledge." (Eph 3, 19).

What more can I say? That this charity is eternal. Or rather, and this is perhaps a better way to put it, it is eternity. So you see that the breadth of God is as great as his length. Would that you could also see that there is not only equality between them, but identity; that one is what the other is; that each one represents nothing less than both together; that both together represent nothing more than each one separately.

Yes, God is eternity, just as he is charity; He is length without tension, breadth without extension. In one way no less than the other, he surpasses the narrow limits of space and time, but by the freedom of his nature, not by the vastness of his substance. Thus he who made everything to measure is himself beyond all measure; and yet, even so, he remains the measure of this same immensity.

What else is God? He is height and depth. By virtue of one, he is higher than all, and by the other, he is lower than all. In fact, it is clear that, in the divine entity, the equilibrium cannot be thrown off balance, neither in one sense nor another; under whatever aspect he is considered, we find him firm in his stability, immutable in his immensity.

Think of height as the power of God and depth as his wisdom. There is an exact correspondence between the two since, as we know, the height of God is as inaccessible as his depth is unfathomable. And this is what St Paul admired when he cried out: "Oh, the depth of the riches of the wisdom and knowledge of God! How mysterious are his judgments, how hidden his ways!" (Rom 11, 33).

Yes, however we consider the perfect unity in God and with God of his wisdom and knowledge, what joy there is for us to cry out with St Paul: "Oh Wisdom full of power, which reaches all things mightily; Oh Power full of wisdom which orders all things sweetly!" (Wisdom 8, 1).

It is but one and the same thing, multiple in its effects, diverse in its actions. And this unique thing is at once length by its eternity, breadth by its charity, height by its power, and depth by its wisdom.

We know all of these things. Do we believe that we have thereby seized them? Not by argument are these matters to be understood, but by holiness, in whatever measure we are able to comprehend what is incomprehensible.

And yet, if it were impossible to understand, the Apostle would not have said "that we must seize,with all the saints." (Eph 3, 18). Consequently, the saints understand. Do you want to know how they do this? If you are a saint, you have already understood and therefore have nothing more to learn; if you are not a saint, you must become one so that your experience will teach you.

It is a saintly disposition of the heart which makes a saint. This includes two sentiments: the holy fear of the Lord and his holy love. The soul which has penetrated all of this is equipped, so to speak, with two sets of arms which allow it to seize, embrace, clasp, and retain. She too can cry out: "I have seized him and I will not let him go!" (Song of Songs 3, 4).

Fear corresponds precisely to that which is high and deep, just as love to that which is long and broad. What is more formidable than an irresistible power? Than a wisdom which can never be deceived? God would be less fearsome if he lacked one or the other. Since this is not the case, never cease to fear him whose eye sees all things and whose arm can do all things. Likewise, what is more loveable than this love which determines the fact that you love and are loved? And yet, when eternity is added on to this love, it becomes still more loveable, for the certainty that it will never end frees it from all suspicion. Love, then, with fidelity and patience, and you will seize the length; extend this love even to your enemies, and you will be in possession of the breadth. Moreover, take care to fear the Lord with as much diligence as possible: then you will understand what is meant by height and depth.

But if you prefer that four dispositions within yourself should correspond to the four terms of our definition of God, you should cultivate admiration, fear, fervor, and patience. It is a fact that the sublime majesty of God should excite our admiration, that the depth of his judgments should awaken our fear. His charity appeals to our fervor, and his eternity to our patience in suffering. Can we admire anything more than when we contemplate the majesty of God? Can we be seized with a greater fear than when we plumb the depths of his wisdom? Can we burn with greater fervor than when we meditate on his charity? Can we offer proof of greater patience and perseverance in love than when we are consumed with desire for this eternal charity? Yes, our perseverance is a kind of prefiguration of this eternity. It is the only virtue which will be rewarded with eternity, or rather, which will restore to man that state of eternity which he has lost. It is the Lord himself who tells us: "He who perseveres to the end will be saved." (Matt 10, 22).

BERNARD ON CHRISTIAN CONDUCT

Introduction: The eighty-sixth *Sermon on the Song of Songs* remains unfinished. Thus it is undoubtedly the last or one of the last texts composed by Bernard. Can these *novissima verba* be considered as a kind of spiritual testament? From the start, he declared his intention to speak as a moralist and to say things related to the conduct of life, *quae ad mores spectant.* We will see the exalted manner in which he accomplished the task.

Already in two preceding sermons, he had begun to speak about the quest of the Word in conjunction with this verse from the Song of Songs: "In my little bed, I have sought him whom I love." We must seek him as he has sought us. (Sermon 84). Why? So that we may become like unto him and thus find a resemblance to him and be made fruitful by him (Sermon 85). After this dogmatic statement, St Bernard turned to the way in which we must seek, and then to how to lead this life of union with God. The last words, borrowed from St Paul, will be a worthy conclusion to this message of light.

Sermon 86

I no longer have to ask myself why the soul seeks the Word. I have said more than enough on the subject. So let us continue our examination of the text, at least with respect to its moral implications. Above all, notice the reserve of the Spouse. I do not know whether there could be

159

anything more gracious in human conduct. It pleases me to take this virtue in my hands, if I may say so, to gather it up from this passage of Scripture like a wonderful flower and offer it to our young brothers. I do not mean that it is not necessary at an advanced age, to guard it with care, like an ornament which remains ever precious; but the charm of this considerate behavior is even more seductive and more noteworthy in one of a tender age. Nothing is more loveable than an adolescent who is modest. In the life and among the traits of a very young man, reserve is the most brilliant of jewels, the sign which does not deceive the loftiest hopes, and the symptom of a good nature. It serves him as a rod lifted against shameful passions, [a rod] which curbs the ardor of his age, prevents inconsiderate actions, and checks revolt. Nothing is better able to scatter vile intentions and all of the infamies that follow in their wake. It is the sister of continence, the surest indication of a simplicity worthy of the dove, the best proof of innocence. A chaste soul has within herself this lamp, always lighted, which immediately dispels the slightest indecent thought lurking in the shadows. Exterminator of evil, active protector of innate purity, it is the glory of the conscience, the guardian of a good reputation, the apparel of life, the seat of power, the first fruits of virtue, the honor of nature, the sign of total honesty. The simple blush which modesty occasionally brings to the cheeks is enough to give the features an infinite grace.

Modesty is a good so inherent in the soul that those who are not afraid to commit evil are still fearful of being seen. The Lord says, in fact: "He who does evil hates the light" (Jn 3, 20). And "those who sleep, sleep during the night; those who get drunk, get drunk during the night" (I Thess 5, 7); they seek obscurity for their works of darkness which are made to remain in the shadows. Yet, there is a great difference: these shocking acts, which such people are not ashamed to commit but to have seen, are not concealed by the modesty of the Spouse, but rather are kept far away from her. The Wise Man also says: "There is a shame which favors sin and a shame which leads to glory" (Sir 4, 25).

Thus the Spouse seeks her Beloved with reserve, since she is in bed and it is night, but it is a glorious reserve and not one that covers sin. She seeks him in order to purify her conscience and be able to offer this testimony: "My glory is the witness of my own conscience" (II Cor 1, 12). "In my little bed, during the night, I have sought him whom my heart loves" (Song of Songs 3, 1). Notice that here we are informed of the place and the moment for this modesty. A chaste soul loves nothing better than solitude. Night and the bed provide the opportunity. If we wish to pray, it is recommended that we retire into our own chambers (Matt 6, 6) so that we will be completely alone. This is by way of precaution because, if we pray in public, human praise could deprive us of the fruit of our prayer. But this Gospel precept also teaches us modesty, whose very nature is to escape such praises and avoid the movements of pride. It is evident that it was specifically from motives of modesty that this counsel was given to us by the One who is the Son and Master of all modesty. There is nothing more unpleasant, especially in a young man, than an ostentatious form of sanctity. And yet, this is the very age which is most favorable and best adapted to the beginnings of religious life. As Jeremiah says: "It is good for a man to bear the yoke from adolescence" (Lam 3, 27). You can prepare a favorable hearing for your prayer if it is preceded by an expression of modesty such as: "I am only a despised child, but I have not forgotten your precepts" (Ps 118, 141).

He who wishes to pray in peace will take into account not only the place, but the time. The moment of rest is the most favorable and when nocturnal sleep establishes a profound silence everywhere, prayer becomes more free and more pure. "Arise during the night, at the beginning of the watch, and pour out your heart like water before the Lord, your God" (Lam 2, 19). With that certainty can prayer rise during the night, when God alone is witness, and the Angel who receives it and goes to present it at the heavenly altar! It is pleasing and luminous, touched by the blush of modesty. It is calm and peaceful when no sound, no cry comes to interrupt. It is pure and sincere when the dust of earthly cares cannot soil it. There is no spectator who can expose it to temptation by his praises and flattery. That is why the Spouse acts with as much wisdom as modesty when she chooses the nocturnal solitude of her chambers to pray, that is to seek the Word, for they are one and the same. You pray badly if, when praying, you seek something other than the Word, or if you do not ask for the object of your prayer in relation to the Word. For everything is in him: the remedies for your wounds, the help which you need, the correction of your faults, the source of your progress. In a word, all that a man can and should wish for. There is no reason to ask the Word for anything other than himself, since he is all things. If we seem to ask, as need be, for certain temporal goods, and if, as we should, we hope to receive them by virtue of our relationship with the Word, it is not so much these things themselves which we ask for as him who is the cause of our prayer. They know it well who have become accustomed to using temporal goods only for the sake of meriting the Word.

However, let us not hesitate to inquire further into the secret of this bed and this nocturnal hour. Perhaps we will find some spiritual mystery which would be profitably exposed to the light of day. If you wish, we will say that the little bed represents our human infirmity and the nocturnal shadows are the image of our ignorance. On this basis, it will be logical and appropriate to appeal against this original dual evil to the aid of the Word who is the power and the wisdom of God. Nothing is more just than to set up force against weakness and wisdom against ignorance. So that this interpretation may leave no doubt in the minds of simple souls, I will remind them of what the prophet has said: "May the Lord sustain him on his bed of pain; you have attended to his sickbed" (Ps 40, 4). So much for the bed. As for the night of ignorance, another psalm speaks very clearly: "Deprived of knowledge and intelligence, they walk in darkness" (Ps 81, 5). This passage designates, without a doubt, the ignorance common to all human beings from their birth. It seems to me that it is this same ignorance of which the

Apostle speaks when he acknowledges having been born into it and gloried in the fact of having been saved from it: "He has saved us from the power of darkness" (Col 1, 13). This is why he says elsewhere: "We are not the sons of night and of darkness" (I Thess 5, 5). And, addressing all of the elect: "Conduct yourselves as children of light" (Eph 5, 8).

ILLUSTRATIONS

The editors of Cistercian Publications
wish to thank the following persons and institutions
for their permission to reproduce the illustrations:

Bodleian Library, Oxford
Elsevier Nederland B.V. uitgevers
Museo del Prado, Madrid
Musées d'Alençon
Osterreichische Galerie, Vienna
M. Pierre Quarré
Zodiaque, Abbaye de la Pierre-qui-Vire

CHRONOLOGY

915 First Abbatial Election, Cluny

975 Second Abbatial Election, Cluny

1026 Abbatial Election, Fleury-sur-Loire

1037 Abbatial Election, Jumièges

1064 Abbaye-aux-Hommes, Caen

1067 Abbatial Election, Saint-Benoit-sur-Loire

1073 Gregory VII, Pope

1079 Birth of Abelard

1085 Death of Gregory VII

1088 Third Abbatial Election, Cluny

1090 Birth of Bernard of Fontaine

1095 Preaching of First Crusade

1098 Foundation of Cîteaux

1099 Paschal II, Pope

1108 Louis VI, the Fat, King of France

1112 Bernard enters Cîteaux

1113 Heloise and Abelard

1115 Foundation of Clairvaux

1118 Foundation of Trois-Fontaines

1118 Gelasius II, Pope

1119 Foundation of Fontenay

1119 Calixtus II, Pope

1121 Foundation of Foigny

1122 Peter the Venerable, Abbot of Cluny

1124 Honorius II, Pope

1130 Innocent II, Pope

1132 Foundation of Rievaulx

1137 Death of Louis VI
Louis VII, King of France

1139 Controversy with Abelard

1141 Council of Sens
Condemnation of Abelard

1143 Death of Innocent II

1145 Bernard in Languedoc
The Cathari

1145 Eugene III, Pope

1146 Bernard preaches Second Crusade at Vézelay

1148 Defeat of Second Crusade at Damascus

1153 Death of Bernard

1153 Death of Eugene III

INDEX

Index

SELECTED BIBLIOGRAPHY

WORKS OF BERNARD

Editions

Leclercq, Jean; H. M. Rochais, and C. H. Talbot, *Sancti Bernardi Opera* (Rome: Editiones Cistercienses, Piazza Tempio di Diana, 14) 1957-

Mabillon, *Opera omnia* (Paris, 1960) reproduced in Migne, J. P., *Patrologia Latina*, (Paris, 1855) vols. 182-83.

English Translations [*recent*]

The complete works of Bernard will appear in the Cistercian Fathers Series (Cistercian Publications). Those already available are dated.

Apology to Abbot William. CF 1 (1970)
On Consideration. CF 37 (1976)
On Conversion. CF 43
On Grace and Free Will. CF 19
On Loving God. CF 13 (1974)
In Praise of the New Knighthood. CF 19
In Praise of the Blessed Virgin Mary. CF 43
On Precept and Dispensation. CF 1 (1970)
On Psalm 90. CF 43
Prologue to the Cistercian Antiphonary. CF 1 (1970)
Letters, 2 vols. CF 28, 57
Life of St. Malachy. CF 16
Sermons on the Song of Songs, 4 vols. CF 4 (1971), CF 7 (1976), CF 31, CF 40
Sermons on the Liturgical Year, 4 vols. CF 10, CF 22, CF 25, CF 34
Occasional Sermons, 2 vols. CF 46, CF 49
Sentences. CS 52
On the Steps of Humility. CF 13 (1974)

Cattani, Georges. *Bernard of Clairvaux* (Dublin, 1966)

Daniel-Rops, Henry. *Bernard of Clairvaux* (New York: Hawthorne, 1964)

Egres, Odo J. *Saint Bernard, His Life and Teaching* (Frosinone, Casamari Abbey, 1961)

James, Bruno Scott. "The Personality of Saint Bernard as Revealed in his Letters," *Collectanea* OCR 14 (1952) 30-34.
. "Self-portrait of a Saint," *The Month* 195 (1953) 235-240.

Knowles, David. "Saint Bernard of Clairvaux, 1090-1153,: *Dublin Review* 227 (1953) 104-121.

Luddy, Ailbe J. *The Life and Teaching of St. Bernard*[2] (Dublin: Gill, 1950)

Merton, Louise (Thomas). The Last of the Fathers: Saint Bernard of Clairvaux and the Encyclical Letter, Doctor Mellifluus. New York: Harcourt Brace; London: Hollis and Carter, 1954.

William of Saint Thierry *et al. St. Bernard of Clairvaux.* Trans Geoffrey Webb and Adrian Walker. London: A. R. Mowbray, 1960.

Williams, Watkin W. *Saint Bernard of Clairvaux.* Manchester: University Press, 1935.

BERNARD'S INFLUENCE

Theology and Teaching

Bouyer, Louis. *The Cistercian Heritage*. London: A. R. Mowbray, 1958.

Gilson, Etienne. *The Mystical Theology of St. Bernard*. London: Sheed and Ward, 1955.

Conflicts with the Cluniacs

Bredero, Adriaan. "The Controversy between Peter the Venerable St. Bernard of Clairvaux," *Studia Anselmiana* 40. Rome, 1956, pp. 53-71.

Knowles, David. *Cistercians and Cluniacs: The Controversy between St. Bernard and Peter the Venerable.* London: Oxford University Press, 1955.

Lang, Ann Proulx. "The Friendship between Peter the Venerable and Bernard of Clairvaux," *Bernard of Clairvaux: Studies Presented in Honor of Dom Jean Leclerq.* CS 23. Washington, D.C.: Cistercian Publications, 1973, pp. 35-53.

Conflict with Scholastics

Little, Edward. "Bernard and Abelard at the Council of Sens, 1140," CS 23, pp. 55-71.

Meadows, Denis. *A Saint and a Half: A New Interpretation of Abelard and St. Bernard of Clairvaux.* New York: Devin and Adair, 1963.

Sommerfeldt, John R. "Abelard and Saint Bernard of Clairaux," *Papers of the Michigan Academy of Science, Arts, and Letters* 46 (1961) 493-501.

. "Bernard of Clairvaux and Scholasticism," *Ibidem* 48 (1963) 265-277.

Bernard and the Papacy

Kennan, Elizabeth T. "The *De consideratione* of St Bernard of Clairvaux and the Papacy in the Mid-twelfth century: A review of Scholarship," *Traditio* 23 (1967) 73-115.

Sommerfeldt, J. R. "Charismatic and Gregorian Leadership in the Thought of Bernard of Clairvaux," CS 23, pp. 73-90.

White, Haydn V. "The Gregorian Ideal and Saint Bernard," *Journal of the History of Ideas* 21 (1960) 321-348.

Iconography of St. Bernard

No work on this subject has been done in English.

Dewez, L. and A. van Iterson. "La lactation de S. Bernard. Légende et iconographie," *Cîteaux* 7 (1956) 165-189.

Durán, M. *Iconografía espanola de San Bernardo.* Poblet, 1953.

Hümpfner, Tilbertus. *Ikonographie des heiligen Bernhard von Clairvaux.* Augsburg, Cologne, Vienna: Dr. Benno Filser Verlag, 1927.

Leclercq, Jean. "Pour l'iconographie de S. Bernard," *Analecta s.o. cist.* 11 (1955) 145-146—lists manuscripts containing depictations of Bernard.

Quarré, Pierre. "L'iconographie de saint Bernard à Clairvaux et les origines de la *vera effigies*," *Melangés saint Bernard.* Dijon, 1953, pp. 342-349.

⸻. *Saint Bernard et l'art des cistercien.* Musée de Dijon, 1953.

Recorded reading, in French, from passages of the works of Bernard of Clairvaux is available under the title, Visages de Saint Bernard (*Encyclopédie sonore* [*Paris: Ducretet-Thomson et Librairie Hachette, 1968*]). *Texts chosen by Jean Leclercq and read by A. Balpêtré.*

THE WORKS OF BERNARD OF CLAIRVAUX

English translations of the works of Bernard of Clairvaux appear in the CISTERCIAN FATHERS SERIES of Cistercian Publications. These new translations are based on the critical Latin edition prepared by Jean Leclercq osb (the author of this volume) and Henri Rochais, and published under the sponsorship of the Order of Cistercians by Editiones Cistercienses, Piazza Tempio di Diana, Rome.

* Available in paper and hard cover
• In preparation: paper and hard cover

CISTERCIAN FATHERS SERIES

Under the direction of the same Board of Editors as the CISTERCIAN STUDIES SERIES, the CISTERCIAN FATHERS SERIES seeks to make available the works of the Cistercian Fathers in good English translations based on the recently established critical editions. The texts are accompanied by introductions, notes and indices prepared by qualified scholars.

In addition to Bernard of Clairvaux, the Cistercian Order in the twelfth century produced writers of sensitivity and spiritual insight. Their works show the vitality of the young order and often manifest the profound influence which St Bernard exercised during his lifetime.

The Works of Aelred of Rievaulx

The Works of William of Saint Thierry

The Works of Guerric of Igny